NELSON
MANDELA

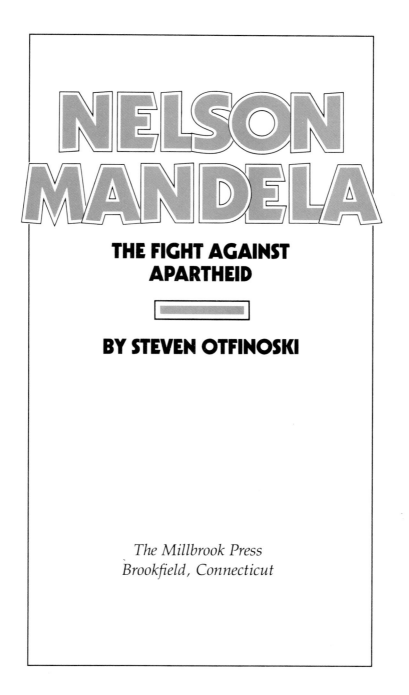

NELSON MANDELA

THE FIGHT AGAINST APARTHEID

BY STEVEN OTFINOSKI

The Millbrook Press
Brookfield, Connecticut

Map by Joe LeMonnier

Photographs courtesy of Impact Visuals: frontis (Paul Weinberg),
pp. 21 (Afrapix/Peter Auf Der Hyde), 27 (IDAF/Eli Weinberg), 35
(Ansell Horn), 47 (IDAF/Eli Weinberg), 50 (IDAF/Eli Weinberg), 55
(IDAF), 64 (IDAF), 78 (IDAF), 96 (Afrapix/Miller), 102 (Afrapix/Miller),
106 (Afrapix/Bosch), 109 (Rick Reinhard), 114 (Afrapix/Rafs
Mayet); Reuters/Bettmann Newsphotos: pp. 10, 69, 87, 93.

Library of Congress Cataloging-in-Publication Data

Otfinoski, Steven.
Nelson Mandela : the fight against apartheid / by Steven Otfinoski.
p.   cm.
Includes bibliographical references (p. 125) and index.
Summary: Describes the life and career of the South African civil
rights worker and his impact on race relations in his country.
ISBN 1-56294-067-8
1. Mandela, Nelson, 1918–   . 2. Civil rights workers—South
Africa—Biography—Juvenile literature.   3. African National
Congress—Biography—Juvenile literature.   4. Political prisoners–
South Africa—Biography—Juvenile literature. [1. Mandela,
Nelson, 1918–   .   2. Civil rights workers. 3. Blacks—South
Africa—Biography. 4. South Africa—Race relations.]   I. Title.
DT1949.M35038   1992
968.06′4′092—dc20
[B]   91-35031   CIP   AC

CONTENTS

NELSON MANDELA

A SHORT WALK
TO FREEDOM

The crowd of black people waiting outside Victor Verster Prison Farm near Cape Town, South Africa, was growing impatient. Some of them had been waiting on this sunny February Sunday since early morning. Three o'clock, the designated time, came and went, and still there was no sign of the man they had come to see released.

Then, at precisely 4:15 P.M., a silver Toyota sedan pulled up the dusty road from the prison farm to the last guard post. A rear door opened, and out stepped a white-haired black man in a dark gray suit. At his side was a handsome black woman in her fifties. The man was tall and gaunt, his face creased with age. The sight of the hundreds of people seemed to startle him. But as he heard their cheers and joyous cries, his spirits rose. He passed through the last barrier, smiling broadly, his right arm raised in a salute and a greeting. His left hand held that of the happy woman by his side.

*Nelson Mandela and wife Winnie raise their arms
in triumph to crowds of supporters as he leaves
Victor Verster Prison Farm on February 11, 1990,
after twenty-seven years of imprisonment.*

Together they marched forward to the point
where the prison road met the highway—a distance of some 70 yards (64 meters). The man
walked firmly and erect, carrying himself with a
dignity rare for a man just released from prison.
He said nothing in response to the cheers, as if his
heart was too full to speak.

Then he climbed into a waiting BMW sedan
and was driven toward Cape Town, 40 miles (64
kilometers) away. The motorcade crawled through
suburban streets lined with well-wishers, most of
them white, holding signs of greeting and calling
his name. Some waved the black, green, and yel-
low flag of the African National Congress, the or-

ganization he helped make famous. Only a short time before, waving such a flag would have been a punishable offense.

The motorcade finally arrived at its destination, Cape Town's City Hall, where a massive crowd, much larger than the one at the prison gate, waited for a glimpse of the man in the BMW. A corridor of police officers helped whisk him through the crowd and into the government building.

By the time he emerged again on the steps of the City Hall, two and a half hours later, the crowd of 50,000 had dwindled to perhaps 20,000. But they were no less enthusiastic at the sight of him. Looking more confident and youthful than he had several hours earlier, the seventy-one-year-old man gazed out at the massive throng and spoke his first word heard in public in twenty-seven years.

"Amandla!" he cried, which means "power" in the African Xhosa language.

As with one voice, the crowd responded "Ngawethu!" ("It is ours!").

"i-Afrika!" cried the man on the steps ("Africa!").

"Mayibuye!" replied the people ("Let it come back!").

"Mayibuye!"

"i-Afrika!"

Then the man began to speak. His words were heard not only by the thousands in the square, but also by tens of millions huddled around television sets in South Africa, Europe, the United States, Australia, and Japan. In measured tones, he talked about the "long, lonely, wasted years" he spent in prison and the commitment to his cause that made it all bearable.

"I stand here before you not as a prophet, but as a humble servant of you, the people," he told them. "Your tireless and heroic sacrifices have made it possible for me to be here today. I herefore place the remaining years of my life in your hands."[1]

He then thanked the many people and groups that had supported him and kept the struggle for black equality in South Africa going while he was in prison. He paid particular tribute to his wife and family, saying, "I am convinced that your pain and suffering was far greater than my own."

His speech continued:

> Today the majority of South Africans—black and white—recognize that apartheid has no future. It has to be ended by our own decisive mass action in order to build peace and security. The mass campaigns of defiance and other actions of our organizations can only culminate in the establishment of democracy . . .
>
> There must be an end to white monopoly of political power and a fundamental restructuring of our political and economic systems to ensure that the inequalities of apartheid are addressed and our society throughout democratized.
>
> Our struggle has reached a decisive moment. We call on our people to seize this mo-

ment so that the process towards democracy is rapid and uninterrupted. We have waited too long for our freedom. We can no longer wait. Now is the time to intensify the struggle on all fronts. To relax our efforts now would be a mistake which generations to come will not be able to forgive. The sight of freedom looming on the horizon should encourage us to redouble our efforts. It is only through disciplined mass action that our victory can be assured. We call on our white compatriots to join us in the shaping of a new South Africa. The freedom movement is a political home for you too . . . Our march to freedom is irreversible. We must not allow fear to stand in our way. Universal suffrage . . . is the only way to peace and racial harmony.[2]

He spoke of the man who had signed his release and called him "a man of integrity." He spoke of peace and harmony and control despite mounting anger and frustration. He called for the release of those hundreds who, like himself, languished in prison for their political beliefs. And when he finished speaking twenty-five minutes later, the crowd cheered long and hard.

After twenty-seven years, six months, and one week in prison, Nelson Mandela was a free man again. South Africa, a land of despair and rage, was, for the moment, filled once more with hope. Mandela's 70-yard walk to freedom had been in reality an epic journey—a journey that started seventy-one years earlier.

A CHIEF'S SON

South Africa is a land of sweeping contrasts. Lying at the southern tip of Africa, it is the most highly developed country on the continent. Yet more than half of its people live in economic squalor. It is a land of unsurpassed physical beauty, from majestic mountains to spectacular beaches. But it is also home to some of the largest and worst slums on earth. It is Africa's richest nation, blessed with untold mineral wealth, fertile soil, and the most advanced modern technology. At the same time, it has been cursed with racial intolerance, institutionalized bigotry, and an oppressive government system that has allowed 5 million whites to control the destiny of 32 million blacks.

The history of modern South Africa is a tale of power and greed, heroism and hatred. Without an understanding of this history, an outsider cannot begin to understand Nelson Mandela—a man who has spent his life trying to alter that history.

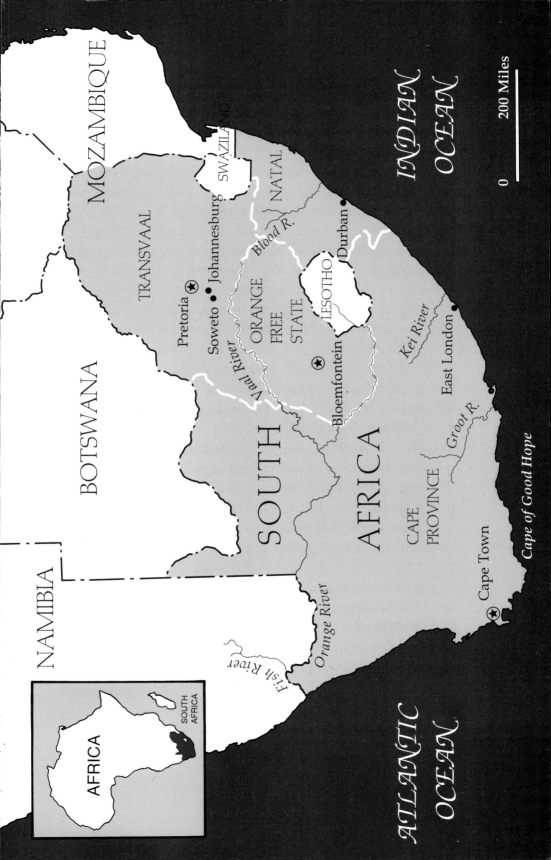

Before 1600, the land that is now South Africa belonged to numerous groups of African peoples. These included the San, Khoi-Khoi, and Bantu-speaking peoples. These various peoples herded their cattle and sheep, farmed in green valleys, and hunted wild animals on vast plains.

The natural beauty of their land and its strategic location did not escape the notice of the Portuguese and Dutch traders who passed around the tip of Africa on ships bound for India. In 1652, the Dutch East India Company established a modest supply station on the coast of what Europeans called the Cape of Good Hope. Here trading ships could replenish their supplies and then continue on their long voyage to the East Indies. The Dutch called this settlement Cape Town. Today it is the second largest city of South Africa.

Five years after their arrival, some of the company's workers were rewarded for agreeing to work so far from their homeland, the Netherlands. They were allowed to settle on the land and start their own farms. These settlers were known as "Boers," Dutch for peasants or farmers.

If the Boers were peasants, they quickly became prosperous ones. By 1700, they had taken over nearly all the good farmland surrounding Cape Town. New European arrivals, encouraged by the East India Company to settle here, moved west into African territory. The white settlers systematically drove out or exterminated the black Africans. By the end of the eighteenth century, the Dutch colony of South Africa had a population of

20,000 whites and 40,000 blacks, many of whom were slaves or servants. However, the vast territory that makes up most of modern South Africa remained in the hands of African peoples, such as the Zulus.

While its colony thrived, the Netherlands itself had been weakened by several European wars. In 1814, the Dutch lost their prized colony to Great Britain. The central conflict in South Africa had until now been between white settlers and native Africans. Now the focus would shift to a growing conflict between whites and whites—the Dutch Boers and their English masters.

The English colonizers took a slightly more liberal attitude toward the Africans than had the Boers. In 1833 they abolished slavery in the British Empire, including South Africa, and gave Africans more rights. This was a crushing blow for the Boers, who had built their economic system on cheap black labor. Furthermore, the British imposed their own government and language on the Boers. Many Boers resisted British influence and prepared to leave Cape Colony and move beyond the power of British rule.

In 1836 they loaded up their ox-drawn wagons and headed north in what has come to be called the "Great Trek." The Boers fought with the African peoples whose homelands they entered. They first clashed with the Ndebele people, whom they defeated and drove off their land. The Zulu people, however, had a strong, well-organized army and bravely defended their land for two long years.

Finally, in December 1838, the Zulus were defeated decisively at the Battle of Blood River. The Zulu chief Dingane ceded much of his land to the Boers, who created the Republic of Natal on South Africa's eastern coast. Yet the Zulus remained an independent people until they were finally conquered by the British in 1879.

As the Boers moved north, the British extended their control east, into lands that were the home of Xhosa-speaking groups. They soon annexed, or took political control of, Natal, but they allowed two other Boer settlements—the Transvaal and the Orange Free State—to operate as independent states. The British looked for a way to coexist peacefully with their Boer neighbors, often at the expense of the Africans, who lost the few rights previously granted them by the British.

The discovery of diamond fields in Kimberley in the Orange Free State in 1870 and the 1879 defeat of the Zulus changed the Boer-British relationship. The Boers no longer needed British protection from surrounding African states. Tensions mounted and eventually erupted into the first Anglo-Boer War in 1880. The Boers fought fiercely and drove the British out of their territory within a year. But when gold was discovered in the same region six years later, hostilities resumed. The Boers denied rights to British gold seekers entering their land. In 1899, the second Boer War broke out; the outcome was very different. Within three years, the Boers were defeated by Britain's superior numbers and firepower.

Black South Africans strongly supported the British in the war and served courageously both in combat and noncombat roles. However, this didn't improve their situation when the war ended and the Boer republics became British colonies. The victors sought to appease their former enemies at the expense of the blacks, and they granted the Boer states self-government. In 1910, the Union of South Africa was formed, joining together all of colonial South Africa under the British flag.

The political union of the British and the Boers only meant further oppression for black Africans. They were second-class citizens at best, with little political and economic power. The Boers, or Afrikaners as they now called themselves, were a proud people who believed they had a God-given mission to rule over the land their ancestors had fought and died for. To them, Africans were simple-minded people whose main purpose in life was to serve them. They were blind to the fact that these same Africans had advanced cultures and civilizations of their own that went back hundreds of years. The defeat of the Boers by the British hardened these views.

In 1914 a group of Afrikaners who were firmly opposed to black rights founded the Nationalist Party of South Africa. Its goal was to uphold the rights and interests of Afrikaners and work toward complete economic and political independence from England.

In this time of turmoil and change, Nelson Rolihlahla Mandela was born in the village of

Qunu, near Umtata, the capital of the Transkei territory, on July 18, 1918. Rolihlahla, his African name, means "one who stirs up trouble" in English. It was a name he would live up to.

The Transkei is a region on the eastern coast of South Africa. Until the late 1800s, the Transkei was the independent homeland of the Xhosa people, who had lived for generations as herders and farmers on the region's fertile grasslands.

By the time of Mandela's birth, the Transkei was part of the Union of South Africa. Like other African areas, it was nominally run by traditional chiefs, but the real power lay in the hands of the white government. These rural people, who had once ruled themselves, were now seen as posing little threat to whites, who mostly left them alone.

Mandela's childhood was a sheltered and peaceful one. He spent his days on the family *kraal*, or farm, with his three sisters, tending to the sheep and cattle and raising pumpkins, beans, and melons.

But the boy's future was to be more ambitious. His father, Henry Gadla Mandela, was a poor but proud chief of the Thembu, a Xhosa-speaking people, and head councillor to the highest leader of his people—the paramount chief. As a member of the royal family, Mandela was expected to one day become a chief like his father and uncles.

At night the impressionable youngster sat around the fire with the elders and thrilled to their stories of the glorious past. They spoke of a golden time, before the white men came from across the

*This humble spot in the Transkei village of Qunu marks
the birthplace of Nelson Mandela. The picture was taken
in 1988, when Mandela's relatives were keeping the plot
of land ready for his anticipated return.*

seas and took their land and rights away. They also
told tales of bravery about Xhosa warriors who
fought the European invaders in the Frontier Wars
of the 1800s. The tall, handsome boy longed to
take up the cause of his people and win back their
natural birthright. But as he grew into adoles-
cence, Mandela came to learn that he could do
more for his people with an education than he
could with a spear.

A sick man whose days were numbered, Henry Mandela sent his son to live at the paramount chief's "great place," Mqekezweni, when the boy was about thirteen. David Dalindyebo, a leading chief and Nelson's uncle, became his legal guardian after his father's death. The grooming process for a future chief had begun.

At his uncle's kraal, Mandela was prepared for the traditional rites of manhood. With other boys his age he went off into the wilderness, armed only with a shield and spear. Nelson dressed in a loincloth and lived off the land for fourteen days. He ate roots and hunted and killed wild animals. On his return, there was a great feast to celebrate his new status among his people.

The next rite for a young Thembu male was marriage. But Nelson saw a different future for himself. He had studied at a local mission school, where he became a devout Christian and a lover of learning. He used his learning and his energies to help others. He was never too busy to assist his sisters with their homework or help a neighbor with a chore. The more he learned in school, the more he realized that the law was one important way he could help his people in their struggle for equal rights.

Nelson attended a training college at the Methodist Mission Center in Healdtown and in 1938 entered the University College at Fort Hare in the village of Alice in the Eastern Cape. Fort Hare was one of the few colleges in South Africa that admitted full-time black students at that time.

A good student, Mandela was well liked and popular. His good looks and charismatic personality helped him make friends easily. One of these new college friends was a brilliant science student, Oliver Tambo. A year older than Mandela, Tambo was also from the Transkei and introduced his new friend to the growing black student protest movement.

There was plenty for black students to protest against in the late 1930s. In 1931, Great Britain granted full independence to South Africa, making it a full member of the British Commonwealth of Nations. Under Prime Minister and National Party founder J.B.M. Hertzog, the Afrikaners set about consolidating their political power. At that time, only blacks in Cape Province were allowed to vote in national elections. In 1936, the government began a series of steps that would gradually remove that right, leaving blacks throughout the country with no voice in government. In addition, segregation acts made special passes mandatory for all blacks and controlled their movements in areas where whites lived.

To protest such unjust laws, Mandela participated in a boycott of a lecture with other students. He was suspended from college near the end of 1940 and told not to return unless he was willing to renounce his political activism.

Mandela returned home to Mqekezweni. The paramount chief had had enough of his young kinsman's wayward ways. Nelson was told to accept the college's ultimatum or forget about his studies. The young man refused to apologize. His guardian, Dalindyebo, thought he had a solution. He decided it was time for Mandela to settle down and get married. That would make him forget both politics and college. According to tribal custom, the guardian made the necessary arrangements.

"He selected a girl, fat and dignified," Mandela later wrote, "*lobola* [customary bride price] was paid, and arrangements were made for the wedding."[1]

But the groom knew that if he settled down to a traditional way of life, he would spend the rest of his days regretting the decision. So Nelson ran away before the wedding and fled north to the Transvaal and the industrial center of Johannesburg. Here, amid the urban squalor of South Africa's largest city, the political education of Nelson Mandela would become complete.

TOWARD AN AFRICAN NATION

Black Africans refer to Johannesburg as "Egoli," or "the city of gold." This is no exaggeration. The city, in northeastern South Africa, lies in the heart of the world's richest gold field. Gold and deposits of other minerals, such as iron and coal, have transformed Johannesburg from a prospectors' camp into a major industrial and commercial center.

Johannesburg and its job opportunities attracted the poor from the overcrowded kraals as well as many foreigners looking for a better life. These included Europeans and Indians and other Asians. Perhaps it is this bewildering ethnic diversity that caused the Boers to refer to the city as "Buiwelstad," or "the devil's town."

For Nelson Mandela, a young man from the country, Johannesburg in 1941 must have appeared both golden and devilish. Around him he saw prosperity and great poverty. While whites lived well in the inner city, blacks and "coloreds" (the South African term for people of mixed race) were forced to live outside the central city in squalid shantytowns called "townships." For the first time in his life, Mandela saw how the white government's racist policies were affecting the lives of all nonwhite peoples, not just blacks but Indians and coloreds as well.

Desperate for work, Mandela, for the only time in his life, went to work for the white establishment. A family friend from Umtata got him a job as a policeman in a gold mine. Armed with a whistle and a heavy club, he was to guard the gate to the compound where the black miners lived. He hoped to be promoted to a clerical position in the mines, but he was forced to leave in order to escape the paramount chief's men, sent to bring him back home.

After taking on a variety of odd jobs, Mandela settled in the township of Alexandra on the northern side of Johannesburg. Here he trained to be a professional boxer and also studied to complete his college degree through a correspondence course.

One day a mutual friend introduced him to Walter Sisulu, a friendly real estate agent, who also hailed from the Transkei. The two men took an immediate liking to each other, although in many ways they were worlds apart. Sisulu was short and stocky, wore glasses, was careless about his dress, and was down-to-earth. Mandela, on the other hand, was tall, handsome, athletic, always immaculately dressed, and slightly aloof.

This rare photo shows the young Mandela in training to be a professional boxer in Johannesburg. He soon abandoned the ring and took up law to fight injustice.

Despite their differences, they shared a commitment to justice and social change that would sustain their friendship for five decades.

Sisulu was a few years older than Mandela and treated him like a younger brother. He found him a room at the home of his fiancée's family and offered him a job working in his agency. He helped pay for Mandela's correspondence college course and, when he graduated, encouraged him to go on to law school part-time at the University of the Witwatersrand. Sisulu even got Mandela a job working in a white law firm to help support himself while he studied.

For the first time in his life, Mandela came into social contact with white people. It was an eye-opening experience. He learned that not all white people in South Africa hated and feared blacks. The lawyers treated him with kindness and respect. There were good white people just as there were good black people, Mandela realized. It was not a person's skin color that mattered, but what he or she was inside that counted.

The lawyers in the firm liked Mandela and encouraged him to stick with his studies and become a lawyer. However, they cautioned him to stay out of politics if he wanted to get ahead. It was one piece of advice that he would not take.

His first brush with the police occurred about this time. Mandela was out with three Indian friends when they boarded an empty streetcar. The white conductor yelled at the Indians for "carrying" the black on board his segregated vehicle.

The three were promptly arrested, and Mandela accompanied them to the police station. Mandela refused to testify against his friends, saying he got on board the streetcar of his own free will. A member of his law firm soon got them all acquitted. It would be the first of many run-ins for Nelson Mandela with the unjust laws of South Africa.

Not all Mandela's friends were male. Another boarder in the house where he lived was a pretty nurse, Evelyn Ntoko Mase, a relative of Walter Sisulu's. The two young people fell in love, and in a short time they were married. The newlyweds moved to Orlando, a new township southwest of the city. Later it would be renamed, taking its new name from the first letters of south-west township—Soweto.

The Mandelas did not lack for friends in their new home. Walter lived close by with his new wife, Albertina, who was also a nurse. Even better, Mandela's old schoolmate Oliver Tambo had arrived in town and was teaching science and mathematics at a nearby school.

If Sisulu was outgoing and gregarious and Mandela regal and dynamic, Tambo was quiet and scholarly. His friends nicknamed him "the Christian" because he had studied to be an Anglican priest.

Sisulu belonged to a political organization called the African National Congress. One evening he invited Mandela and Tambo to join him at a meeting. The two men liked what they saw and heard, and they quickly enrolled as members themselves.

The African National Congress, or ANC, was already thirty-two years old when Mandela joined it in 1944. South Africa's oldest liberation organization, it was founded by four black lawyers who modeled it after the democratic Congress of the United States. These men were not wild-eyed revolutionaries but committed political activists who sought to bring about change in their country through the kind of nonviolent protest pioneered by Mohandas K. Gandhi. Although Gandhi is most famous for his use of civil disobedience to gain independence for his native India from Great Britain, in the early 1900s he lived and worked as a lawyer in South Africa. Gandhi's first experiment in nonviolent protest was aimed at the South African government for its poor treatment of Indian immigrants.

The ANC set out to apply these same techniques to the liberation of all nonwhite people in South Africa and end the detested color bar that made them second-class citizens. The ANC had been a vibrant organization at first; but as the years passed, it lost much of its inspiration. Newer, more effective groups, such as the Industrial and Commercial Workers Union and the All-African Convention, drained its membership in the 1920s and 1930s. In 1942, it was further weakened when a splinter group broke away and formed the African Democratic Party.

By the time Mandela and Tambo joined the ANC, it was suffering a mid-life crisis. The three friends believed that what the ANC needed were fresh ideas and a renewed sense of commitment. To accomplish this, they helped form a Youth League within the ANC. In their statement of purpose they claimed that "the Congress Youth League must be the brains-trust and power station of the spirit of African nationalism."[1]

In the Congress Youth League, Nelson Mandela found his life's work. Here was an organization where he could put all his energies to work for the betterment of his fellow Africans. At first, both he and Sisulu saw this as an African—not a national—goal. Whereas Tambo believed that all South Africans, including whites, could be part of the ANC's work, his two friends wanted it to stay a black organization. In their policy statement of 1948 they claimed that "Africa was, has been and still is a Black Man's continent . . . Although conquered and subjugated, the Africans have not given up, and they will never give up their claim and title to Africa."[2]

Such a message was received with hope and optimism in post–World War II Africa. The war had ended in victory for the United States and its Allies and utter defeat for fascist Japan and Germany. South Africa had fought on the Allied side, and Africans across the continent looked forward to their own liberation from colonial rule.

South Africa, however, was no longer a colony. The enemy here was within—the white minority government, which had become completely independent from Britain in 1931. This minority, unfortunately, would only be strengthened by the postwar economic boom and renewed investments from overseas. But this was not yet apparent to many black South Africans.

As the war ended, Johannesburg saw the largest parade in its history. ANC supporters took their place in the long victory march. With one voice, 20,000 Africans shouted their slogan, "Let's finish the job!" What they meant was, "Let's finish the fight for liberation here at home, just like we did abroad."

But these words took on a more ominous meaning for the white Afrikaner Nationalist Party. They were about to bring down the curtain on what limited black rights remained in South Africa in a way that would stun the world.

A LAND DIVIDED

People who don't know the history of South Africa may assume that apartheid, the country's legalized policy of racial segregation, had existed from the beginning of white settlement. But while racial discrimination has been a part of South Africa for three and a half centuries, apartheid did not actually become a reality until 1948.

In May of that year the Afrikaner Nationalist Party came into power. The original Nationalist Party had been formed back in 1914 to represent the political interests of Afrikaners. In 1934, it fused with the more moderate South African Party to fight Depression conditions, forming the United Party. However, some conservatives refused to go along. They joined the "Purified" Nationalist Party, headed by Daniel Malan. Under Malan's leadership this new Nationalist Party grew in power. The split between the two groups widened during World War II, when the moderates wanted to support England and the United States, which the country eventually did. Some conservative Afrikaners felt a stronger allegiance to Nazi Germany, while many others were simply antipathetic to the British cause.

In the 1948 election, the Nationalists beat the more liberal, ruling United Party by a narrow margin. In his victory speech, Daniel Malan, the new prime minister, declared, "Today South Africa belongs to us once more . . . and may God grant that it will always remain our own."[1]

To ensure this, the Afrikaners decided to codify racial prejudice into a system that would carry the full weight of the law. "Apartheid" means apartness in Afrikaans (the derivative of Dutch spoken by Afrikaners). And the apartheid laws were established to do just that—keep the whites and blacks apart, politically, economically, and socially. There had been segregation laws earlier in South Africa, including the Land Act of 1913 and the Native Urban Areas Act of 1923, both of which limited where blacks could live. But the laws of apartheid went much further, institutionalizing racism on a level rarely seen before in modern times.

Apartheid prohibited blacks from attending white schools, living in the same neighborhoods as whites, or marrying someone of another racial group. Blacks were segregated not only from whites, but from other nonwhite groups, such as Asians and coloreds, as well. Under the Population Registration Act of 1950, the entire population of

The squalor and poverty of the black townships is captured in this picture of a Soweto shantytown. Millions of black South Africans were condemned to such living conditions by the apartheid system.

South Africa was divided into rigid racial classes. Every citizen was given documents specifying his or her racial classification. These had to be carried at all times. A complex caste system evolved, with whites on top, followed by Asians, coloreds, and blacks.

Apartheid not only robbed nonwhite South Africans of the few remaining rights they had, it also destroyed the very fabric of their family and social life. Thousands of workers were forced to move out of white neighborhoods into already overcrowded townships. Many of these people had jobs in cities such as Johannesburg, where they now couldn't live, and had to commute long hours to and from work each day. Children often wouldn't see their parents except on weekends or holidays.

The reaction of the ANC's Youth League to apartheid was one of shocked anger. Nelson Mandela called it an "insane policy" and called for nationwide civil disobedience.

While the "old guard" that still ran the ANC rejected the new activism of its Youth League, Mandela and his friends appealed to thousands of blacks who felt a similar call to action. In December 1949, Walter Sisulu was appointed secretary-general of the Congress and was paid the princely sum of five pounds a month in salary, the equivalent today of about twelve dollars. Mandela, following his friend up the ladder, was elected to the group's National Executive Committee.

A landmark in the fight against apartheid took place on May 1, 1950. This May Day, traditionally a day to honor the workers of South Africa, was chosen as a day of national strike by the Youth League. Police attacked the strikers; eighteen blacks were killed and more than thirty were injured.

"The day was a turning-point in my life," Mandela later wrote, "both in understanding through first-hand experience the ruthlessness of the police, and in being deeply impressed by the support African workers had given to the May Day call."[2]

He also was impressed by the support of Indians and Communists in the protests that followed the national strike. Mandela now realized that the anti-apartheid struggle was one that black Africans couldn't and shouldn't try to win alone. South Africans of all races and backgrounds saw the injustices of the system and were needed to help change it.

The government struck back with two more laws that would become central pillars of its apartheid policy. The Groups Areas Act called for separate residential areas for each racial group. Any remaining black neighborhoods in white urban regions were completely eradicated under the guise of "slum removal." (Since most blacks had already been relocated to reserves and townships, the groups most affected by this law were coloreds and Indians.) The Suppression of Communism

Act empowered the government to ban all Communists from political organizations and put them in prison for up to ten years.

South Africa, like many Western nations in the postwar years, was fervently anti-Communist. But fear of Communism had little to do with this new law. In reality, there were only two thousand card-carrying Communists in all of South Africa at the time, and they offered little threat to the government. As defined by this new act, however, a "Communist" was any person who attempted to bring about "any political, industrial, social or economic change within the Union . . . by unlawful acts."[3] This gave the government the legal right and power to suppress every dissenter in South Africa, regardless of his or her political beliefs.

While the ANC and its leadership did not reject the support of Communists and even admired some Communist doctrine, it was not Communist itself and did not espouse a Communist revolution in South Africa. The Suppression of Communism Act ironically brought the ANC and the Communist Party into a closer alliance, but one that would not last.

Mandela was elected national president of the Youth League in late 1950. In a speech a year later, he told the membership that "the problem of the Youth League and ANC today is the maintenance of full dynamic contact with the masses."[4] To solve this problem, President Mandela traveled across the country, often with Tambo, walking into towns and villages and talking to the people. They knocked on doors and sometimes had them slammed in their faces. Other times, they found people eager to listen and learn about the ANC and its goals.

On April 6, 1952, the Afrikaners celebrated the three hundredth anniversary of the Dutch landing at Cape Town. The same day, thousands of black Africans prayed for a return of the freedom they had enjoyed before the whites came to their land. As volunteer-in-chief of the Defiance Against Unjust Laws Campaign, Mandela arrived in Cape Town to sign up volunteers for a series of carefully planned demonstrations.

One white South African recalled his first glimpse of Mandela in the street: "I saw this magnificent figure of a man, immaculately dressed. Not just blacks, but whites, including white women, were turning to admire him."[5]

It was this same charisma that led one friend to comment that Mandela possessed an "animal magnetism that attracts the masses like pollen attracts bees."[6]

This quality did not escape the notice of the white authorities. On June 26, 1952, Mandela spoke at a political meeting past the curfew hour of 11 P.M. He was arrested by the police and spent his first night in jail. In the morning, the prisoners were fed breakfast. Mandela noticed that an Indian colleague had coffee, bread, and jam on his tray, while he got only porridge and water. When he brought this to the guard's attention, Mandela was told to "shut up and eat."

Prison was tolerable, but there was another kind of confinement that was harder to bear for the anti-apartheid fighters. Banning is a peculiar form of South African punishment. A person who is banned is prevented from leaving the town or neighborhood where he or she lives and is prohibited from attending any gathering or, in many cases, even being seen in the company of more than one person at a time. Banning was an effective way for the white government to isolate activist leaders from their supporters and weaken their power.

In December 1952, Mandela was elected deputy president of the ANC, and Zulu chief Albert Luthuli was elected president. Although an older man, Luthuli was the first ANC president to sympathize with the younger leadership and give his support to their protest campaign. "I have joined my people in the new spirit that moves them today, the spirit that revolts openly and boldly against injustice,"[7] Luthuli told the Congress. Both men were promptly banned for six months for their part in the Defiance Campaign. They, along with many others who were banned, took the risk of continuing their activities illegally, knowing that if they were caught they would go to prison.

If the government thought these efforts to squash protest would work, they were sadly mistaken. Banning, arrests, and violence only strengthened the ANC. Within a few short years its membership swelled from 7,000 to more than

100,000. The United Nations, impressed by the ANC's peaceful protests, set up a special commission to study apartheid. It was the first sign that apartheid was not only dividing the people of South Africa, but cutting off the white minority government from the rest of the Western world as well.

While Mandela was busy pursuing political activism, he did not completely neglect his legal career. Amid the turmoil of the Defiance Campaign, he formed a law partnership with Oliver Tambo, who had abandoned teaching for law. While there were black lawyers in South Africa, there had never before been a black law partnership. The two friends established their office in an Indian-owned building in Johannesburg and set to work defending nonwhites in apartheid cases, as well as those with other legal problems. They made a good team. Tambo's quiet, thoughtful style complemented Mandela's more passionate, driven personality.

As a black lawyer, Mandela's understanding of the system of oppression grew. "We became aware of the fact that as attorneys we often dealt with officials whose competence and attainments were no higher than ours, but whose superior position was maintained and protected by a white skin,"[8] he later wrote.

If Mandela's professional and political life was satisfying, his home life was not. The Mandelas had three children by now—two boys, Thembi and Makgatho, and a girl, Makaziwe. Mandela was a good father, but Evelyn, who was not a political person, resented the time he spent away from the family attending protests, demonstrations, and meetings. She wanted him to forget about politics and put all his efforts into his law practice. As time went on, the couple grew further and further apart.

Meanwhile, the white authorities were doing their best to silence this powerful leader. Mandela no sooner served out his six-month ban, in June 1953, than the government slapped another one on him, this time for two years. Unable to leave his home outside Johannesburg, he was forced to temporarily resign from the ANC.

"I found myself treated as a criminal—an unconvicted criminal," he later wrote. "I was not allowed to pick my company, to frequent the company of others, to participate in their political activities, to join their organizations . . . I was made, by the law, a criminal, not because of what I had done, but because of what I stood for, because of what I thought, because of my conscience."9

In an address read by a friend in his absence at the ANC Annual Conference in the Transvaal, Mandela ended his remarks with these words from Indian leader Jawaharlal Nehru, a follower of Gandhi: "You can see that 'there is no easy walk to freedom.' "

For Nelson Mandela, and those who followed him, the walk to freedom would become increasingly difficult.

THE LONGEST
TRIAL

On June 25, 1955, the ANC, together with other anti-apartheid groups in what was called the Congress Alliance, held a historic meeting southwest of Johannesburg. They called it the Congress of the People. The most historic event of this important occasion was the issuing of a Freedom Charter, written in committee and approved by Mandela and other ANC leaders.

The opening of the charter was as bold a statement of objective as the American Declaration of Independence, written nearly two hundred years earlier. "We the people of South Africa," it read, "declare for all our country and the world to know; that South Africa belongs to all who live in it, black and white, and that no government can justly claim authority unless it is based on the will of all the people."[1]

The charter went on to call for a nonracial state where all South Africa's people would share in the country's resources and wealth. It became a vital document that would remain the cornerstone of the ANC's—and Nelson Mandela's—credo for years to come. While the society the Freedom Charter envisioned was still a distant dream, it gave the ANC and its allies something that would often be in short supply in the difficult years ahead—hope.

As for Nelson Mandela, the personal freedom he hoped for was not to be forthcoming. His two-year ban no sooner ran out at the end of 1955 than the government imposed another one on him— this ban for five years. Separated from his friends, Mandela was also now estranged from his wife. Evelyn had gone to Natal ostensibly to study midwifery. In reality, this was the start of a formal separation for the troubled couple.

The new year brought more protests and demonstrations and more police violence. The government's latest ploy to strengthen apartheid was to establish seven so-called "homelands," where blacks would live in supposed self-rule. Formerly called reserves, these homelands were in actuality glorified ghettos run by puppet chiefs who followed orders dictated by the white government. By enticing blacks to live in these isolated "African states," the government effectively cut them off from any hope of meaningful political participation in South Africa. In a few years, the white government would initiate a new policy whereby the homelands were promised power and eventual independence. But the cruel fact remained that the homelands were too small and economically dependent for the blacks assigned to them to ever serve as more than, as one author puts it, "labour dormitories for the white South African economy and as convenient dumping grounds for blacks whose labour was not needed by white employers."[2]

One of the largest homelands was Mandela's own Transkei, soon to be ruled by his relative, Chief Kaiser Matanzima. Mandela's reaction to the homelands policy, later recorded in a magazine article, was blunt. He called it politically a swindle and economically an absurdity.

In the early morning hours of December 5, 1956, Mandela was sleeping soundly in his Orlando home when he was suddenly awakened by a loud knocking at the door. The dreaded "knock at the door" was something known and feared in many a totalitarian state—the police coming under cover of darkness to arrest someone. It would be a sound heard all too often throughout the black neighborhoods of South Africa in the dark days ahead.

Mandela was arrested on charges of "high treason" for advocating revolution to establish a "people's democracy." In the upside-down world of the Nationalist government, this was viewed as Communist treason.

He was in good company. Tambo and Sisulu greeted him in the police van that took them to the Fort, Johannesburg's infamous old prison. Here they found many more colleagues and allies who had also been arrested in a huge security sweep. Within a few days the total of those arrested was

156. Of this number 105 were black, 23 white, 21 Indian, and 7 colored. They included not only lawyers and political leaders, but also teachers, housewives, and laborers. Ironically, Mandela, who while "at large" was isolated from his closest friends, was now able to talk and share freely with them for the first time in years—in a prison cell.

Six days before Christmas the 156 defendants, all members of the Congress Alliance, went on trial. The opening court session was a mixture of the festive and the comic. Crowds of supporters jammed the court hall singing liberation songs. When a microphone failed to work, the court was abruptly adjourned while onlookers laughed and cheered.

The next day the proceedings took a grim turn. The defendants were placed in a wire cage, and when their supporters protested, the police fired on the crowd, injuring twenty-two. When the defense lawyers threatened to walk out, the cage was finally removed. Even in the unjust system of the Nationalist government, 156 people accused of nonviolent crimes could not be kept in jail indefinitely. Bail was made and the accused were released.

This was an extremely troubling time for the thirty-eight-year-old Mandela. His marriage was breaking up, he had little money because his working hours were restricted, and he was on trial for serious crimes that could put him behind bars for life if he was convicted. It was at this low point in his life that Mandela met the person who would restore his spirits and become his partner and soul mate in his mission.

The 156 defendants in the infamous Treason Trial pose
for a group picture. Note the mixture of races. Mandela
is in the center of the third row from the bottom.

Shortly before his arrest, he was buying food in a Johannesburg deli when Tambo and his fiancée Adelaide Tsukudu drove up with a friend of Adelaide's. She was Winnie Nomzamo Madikizela, a pretty twenty-year-old social worker. In the Xhosa language, Nomzamo means "one who strives or goes through trials." This name would take on a special poignancy for Winnie in the years ahead.

She was impressed with this tall, handsome, totally committed but thoroughly charming older man. Her shyness prevented her from saying much, however, and she didn't think he even noticed her.

Some weeks later, during the Treason Trial, Winnie was surprised when Mandela called her up and invited her to Sunday lunch. She accepted, and he took her to a favorite Indian restaurant. Winnie tried hot Indian curry for the first time with some trepidation, to her date's amusement. Later he took her for a drive into the country, and they walked. If romance was on his mind, it took a backseat to politics. He asked her if she would raise money for the Treason Trial Defendants Defense Fund. The fund was set up to help meet legal fees and aid the defendants' families. "If you are looking for some kind of romance," Winnie told one reporter about their early relationship, "you won't find it."[3]

Winnie came from a rather well-to-do family in the Transkei. Although she was well educated, she was not a political activist. Through this charismatic man she would come to see the world through new eyes.

Mandela's divorce from Evelyn finally went through, and on a picnic in March 1957 he proposed marriage to Winnie. In accepting, she accepted not only the man but also his cause. They were married a year later, in June 1958. According to tradition, the ceremony was held in Winnie's home village of Bizana. Because Mandela was still on trial for treason and was also still serving his ban, he had to make a special appeal to the government to attend his own wedding. He was granted a four-day leave from Johannesburg.

The wedding took place in a Methodist church. Although the bride and bridegroom were Protestant, elements of traditional African ceremony were mixed in with the Christian service. One of these traditions said the wedding cake must be cut at the bridegroom's home before his elders. There wasn't time to go to Nelson's home, so the couple returned to Johannesburg with their cake intact and uneaten. Winnie kept the cake, waiting for the day when they could go back to the Transkei together. Little did she know how long she would have to wait for that. In all those years, she claims the cake has never crumbled.

The newlyweds moved into Mandela's modest three-room house in Orlando. Little more than a shack by white standards, the home was definitely upscale for the black township. Unlike many black homes, it had hot running water, electricity, and an indoor bathroom.

Meanwhile, the Treason Trial dragged on. After a year's adjournment, during which the defense lawyers and the prosecution built their case,

A very happy Nelson and Winnie on their wedding day in June 1958. Nelson, on trial for treason, had to apply for special permission to leave Johannesburg to attend the wedding.

the trial officially opened in the administrative capital city of Pretoria.*

It was the start of a strange, rather surreal routine. Each afternoon after the day's proceedings, many of the 156 defendants would leave the courtroom to return home to Johannesburg, 90 miles (145 kilometers) away. Each morning they would make the long journey back to the courtroom to again enter the dock. Mandela and Tambo even managed to resume their law practice parttime.

Wanting to strengthen its case, the court dismissed charges against 61 of the accused, including Oliver Tambo and Albert Luthuli. Mandela and Sisulu were among those still on trial. "It is with mixed feelings that I received the news of my release," Luthuli later said. "The truth is that I would be happier to see the whole thing through with my comrades."[4]

The unusual length of the proceedings, now in their second year, was beginning to have an adverse effect on the government. In a United Nations session, many countries, including the United States, issued a resolution that openly criticized apartheid in South Africa for the first time.

In September 1958, Winnie Mandela's baptism in political reality was completed. The dreadful "knock at the door" came in the night, and this time Winnie was the one arrested. She had partici-

* South Africa is perhaps the only country in the world with three capitals— Cape Town, where the laws are made; Pretoria, where the government has its headquarters; and Bloemfontein, center of the judicial system.

pated with thousands of other black women in demonstrations against new pass laws. These pass laws demanded that nonwhite South Africans carry documents approving their movements in areas where only whites could live. Winnie, pregnant with her first child, spent two terrible weeks in jail. She believed she would have lost the baby if not for the tender care and comfort of her friend Albertina Sisulu. The child, a girl, was later born healthy and named Zenani (Zeni), which means "what have you brought?" in the Xhosa tongue.

The hospital where Winnie worked was nervous about her political activities and fired her. She got a job as a social worker with the Johannesburg Child Welfare Society. With Nelson still on trial and with a daughter to support, Winnie needed to keep working.

In January 1959, feeling the pressure of international criticism, the government dropped its case against more of the defendants. Now only 30 of the original 156 defendants remained on trial. Mandela and Sisulu were, of course, a part of this select group.

The government's case rested on trying to prove that the anti-apartheid leadership was set on overthrowing the government and turning South Africa into a Communist state. Ironically, the younger membership of the ANC were at the same time trying to remove the Communist Party from the Alliance, but for different reasons. They wanted to make the Alliance all black and more militant. They were reacting against Mandela and his friends, who now were the top leadership in the ANC. But with these leaders on trial, the organization was too weak to deal with internal dissension. In April 1959 the inevitable happened. The young militants, led by Robert Sobukwe, a university lecturer only a few years younger than Mandela, left the ANC and formed the Pan-Africanist Congress (PAC). PAC espoused armed revolution as the best solution to apartheid. The ANC stuck to its moderate, nonviolent stand, but the formation of PAC sounded an ominous note of discord amid black harmony.

Nelson Mandela was facing other problems. Quoting the Group Areas Act, the government told him and Tambo that they could no longer practice law in Johannesburg but had to move their office to the township, closer to where they lived. The two men saw this ploy for what it was—an attempt to get them to abandon their practice altogether. They stubbornly refused, and in the face of further prosecution Mandela continued to go to his office and work on nights and weekends.

The year 1960 heralded in a new decade and a new hope for the peoples of Africa. The colonial empires of the last half century were crumbling. Ghana, formerly called the Gold Coast, had become the first black colony to win its independence from Great Britain three years earlier. The fever of freedom was spreading throughout much of the continent.

But in South Africa a bad situation was about to grow worse. A tragedy was about to occur that would stun the world and irrevocably change the course of Nelson Mandela's life.

FIGHTING FIRE
WITH FIRE

Before March 21, 1960, few people outside South Africa had ever heard of Sharpeville, a quiet town 30 miles (48 kilometers) south of Johannesburg. On that day, PAC leader Robert Sobukwe organized a massive protest against the same pass laws Winnie Mandela had demonstrated against two years earlier. Sobukwe wanted to beat the rival ANC, which had scheduled its own demonstration for ten days later. As a result, the PAC demonstration was poorly organized.

On that fateful morning thousands of blacks gathered outside the Sharpeville police station. They carried no passes and expected to be arrested and jailed. Reporters called the crowd "amiable." Many people had come along simply out of curiosity. As the crowd grew larger, the nervous Sharpeville police called for reinforcements from a neighboring town. Soon there were two hundred police officers on the scene. When some of the demonstrators threw stones at them, a number of

*The grim aftermath of the Sharpeville massacre, in
which white police killed sixty-nine blacks, is seen here.
Many people were shot in the back as they ran away.
This tragic event helped convince Mandela that nonviolent protest would not end apartheid.*

officers opened fire with shotguns directly into the
crowd. In twenty seconds, 743 bullets were fired.

A friend of Winnie Mandela's who was there
later described the scene: "The people were laugh-
ing and chatting. It was like a holiday. Then suddenly I heard these shots, shots, shots, shots.
Everyone was screaming and pushing madly to
get away but the police kept firing. There was dead
people lying on the ground everywhere. I couldn't
look any more. I rushed to my car and drove like a
mad woman."[1]

When the smoke cleared, sixty-nine blacks lay dead, including eight women and ten young children. Many were shot in the back as they ran. More than a hundred people were injured. Some of these died later in the hospital.

News of the Sharpeville massacre swept like wildfire around the world. There had been plenty of violence against blacks in South Africa before this, but the cold brutality at Sharpeville was something new. Africans, particularly the young, rose up in bitter rage, and riots erupted in dozens of cities and towns. The government announced an immediate state of emergency to suppress the violent response. Public meetings were forbidden, and a detention law was passed that made it legal to hold anyone in jail for up to ninety days without a trial. Two thousand political activists were promptly rounded up and jailed. Mandela and the other thirty Treason Trial defendants were held at the Fort in Johannesburg. The government feared their influence over the already angry black population.

Then, on April 8, the South African Parliament voted 128 to 16 to ban the ANC and PAC as "unlawful organizations." Oliver Tambo immediately fled the country and went to Great Britain, where he established ANC headquarters in exile in London. He later moved to Zambia, one of the newly independent African states to the north. Here he remained in exile for the next thirty years.

Back in Pretoria, Mandela and his fellow prisoners lived under intolerable conditions. Five men were put into one cramped cell with a bucket on the floor for a toilet. They ate porridge and slept on mats ridden with lice. While in prison, Mandela heard that Winnie was pregnant with their second child.

In August, still in detention, Mandela was asked to testify at the Treason Trial. In the four years of the trial, he had plenty of time to plan his defense. His testimony was eloquent, righteous, and long, filling 441 pages of the court's official record.

If Sharpeville brought the struggle against apartheid to the world's attention, Mandela's testimony at his trial gave a face to that struggle. Before he was a local political activist; now he was an international spokesman for human rights.

When one of the three judges accused him of being anti-white, Mandela responded: "We are not anti-white, we are against white supremacy, and in struggling against white supremacy, we have the support of some sections of the European population."[2]

By the end of August the state of emergency was lifted, and the thirty defendants were allowed to return home. But Winnie would see little of her busy husband until the Christmas holiday and court adjournment. On December 23, she gave birth to their second daughter, Zindzi.

Three months later, the state concluded its long-winded argument. And on March 29, 1961, Mandela and his co-defendants filed quietly into the dock to hear the court's verdict. The senior judge announced in grave tones that the state had failed, in four years of proceedings, to prove that the ANC and its leaders were Communist or Communist-inspired. "You are found not guilty and discharged," he told the elated defendants. It was a day of celebration for the anti-apartheid forces. They left the courtroom carrying their chief lawyer on their shoulders and singing as a crowd of supporters rushed to welcome them.

But this was also a day for serious reevaluation. Nelson Mandela and the ANC had clung to the fervent belief that nonviolent resistance could make a difference in South Africa. The horror of Sharpeville and its brutal aftermath shook that belief to its foundations. In an interview shortly after, Mandela said, "If the government reaction is to crush by naked force our nonviolent struggle, we will have to reconsider our tactics."[3]

Peaceful resistance had worked for Gandhi in India, and at that very moment Martin Luther King, Jr., and his followers were using it effectively to overturn racism in the American South. But Great Britain, Gandhi's colonial foe, and the United States were lands of laws that ultimately upheld individual rights. South Africa had no such democratic tradition. It was now painfully clear to Mandela that the white government would not relinquish or share power until it was forced to.

Mandela and his ANC colleagues were not terrorists. The taking of human life was repugnant to them and went against everything they stood for. They also realized that a civil war, fought by guerrilla tactics, would tear the country apart and make any later reconciliation with white South Africans impossible.

The road they decided to take was one of carefully planned industrial sabotage. If such acts of destruction could frighten off other countries investing in South Africa, the white government's economic system would be seriously weakened, Mandela reasoned. This could lead the government to reassess its policies and voluntarily end apartheid.

International disagreement over South Africa's racial policy, however, was not yet strong enough to affect any one country's doing business with the white regime. UN resolutions were one thing; economic sanctions that would affect a country's pocketbook were quite another. Mandela's tactics, whatever one thinks of them, were doomed to failure at this moment of history.

On March 25, 1961, the Congress Alliance held a special All-African Conference at Pietermaritzburg in Natal. The 1,400 delegates had come together to protest the imminent formation of the "Republic of South Africa." The nation was about to declare its complete independence from the British Commonwealth. To the Congress Alliance, this would be no "republic," but the white supremacist state the Nationalist Party had been working toward for decades.

Amid the meeting, Nelson Mandela appeared on the platform, unannounced. He wore no shoes, to symbolize his solidarity with the common people. Mandela delivered his first public speech since the pre-ban days of 1952. The crowd went wild as he called for a general strike on May 31, the day of "independence." A National Action Council was immediately elected to organize the strike and other demonstrations. Mandela was the unanimous choice to head the council. It would be the last time he would appear in public for nearly thirty years.

But the strike, effective as it would be, was not where Mandela's heart now lay. To launch his program of carefully controlled sabotage, he, Walter Sisulu, and Joe Slovo, head of the Communist Party, set up a secret organization called Umkonto We Sizwe, or, in English, Spear of the Nation. The Spear's targets would be power plants, communication lines such as telephones and railroads, and other industrial sites. Mandela made it clear that these sites were to be bombed only when empty. There could be no loss of life.

Although the government as yet knew nothing of his plans, Mandela realized he would not remain at large for long. With the ANC now officially outlawed, he knew he would be arrested again in a matter of days or weeks if he continued his political activities. Mandela made the difficult decision to go "underground" and disappear from public view. "There comes a time," he later wrote, "when a man is denied the right to live a normal life, when he can only live the life of an outlaw because the government has so decreed."4

So he temporarily said good-bye to his wife and children and left home. He lived on the run, always staying one step ahead of the police. He established his headquarters at a modest house on a small farm in Rivonia, an outer suburb of

Johannesburg. To avoid suspicion, the saboteurs grew produce and sold it by the roadside. Some of their best customers were police officers!

When Mandela was at the farm, Winnie would sometimes meet him there for a few precious days. Most of the time he traveled around the country in disguise, meeting with friends, the press, and other underground leaders. He became a master of disguise, posing at different times as a window cleaner, mechanic, errand boy, night watchman, priest, and even a tribal healer. One of his most useful disguises was that of a chauffeur. Dressed in a white dust coat and black peaked chauffeur's cap, Mandela could travel freely around Johannesburg, without arousing suspicion. The authorities weren't the only ones fooled by this disguise.

One day Winnie was driving in downtown Johannesburg and pulled up alongside a car at a traffic light. The chauffeur turned and winked at her. Winnie realized to her surprise that it was her husband behind the wheel! She smiled but said nothing to him and a moment later drove away. They both knew that any sign of recognition might be seen by the police or an informant. No place was safe.

Another time, Mandela was waiting on a street corner for a car to pick him up. When it didn't appear at the appointed time, he began to worry. All at once, a black security police officer started toward him. The officer looked directly into Mandela's eyes. The fugitive saw that despite his chauffeur's uniform, he had been recognized. Then, at the moment he expected to be arrested, the officer winked at him and gave him the ANC thumbs-up salute. The policeman walked away. Mandela breathed a sigh of relief. An enemy had turned out to be a friend!

Mandela's elusiveness led the South African press to dub him the Black Pimpernel. The name came from the classic adventure novel *The Scarlet Pimpernel*, about a daring nobleman in disguise who helped people in trouble during the French Revolution. The nickname only further frustrated the authorities, who watched Mandela's reputation grow with each day he remained at large.

On December 16, 1961, the Spear of the Nation struck for the first time with twenty-three separate acts of sabotage. Bombs exploded in three major cities. The following morning the group formally announced itself to the world. "The time comes in the life of any nation when there remain only two choices—submit or fight," they wrote in a formal statement. "That time has now come in South Africa. We shall not submit, and we have no choice but to hit back by all means in our power, in defense of our people, our future and our freedom."[5]

But Mandela and his friends were better political organizers than saboteurs. "They hadn't the foggiest idea how to blow things up," wrote Mary Benson, who would later become Mandela's first biographer. "It was very amateurish and desperate. But they felt people were getting very impatient, that it was important to try to lead the anger into a sort of violence that does not harm people."[6]

According to Spear leader Joe Slovo: "Among the lot of us we did not have a single pistol. No one we knew had ever engaged in urban sabotage with home-made explosives."[7] The bombs were put together in one member's kitchen. The timing device was constructed from the tubing in a ballpoint pen. One saboteur died when a bomb misfired. To make matters worse, the organization's security was weak and made it easy prey to the army of police informants that infiltrated its ranks.

In January 1962, Mandela sneaked out of South Africa for the first time and showed up at a Pan-African Freedom Conference in Ethiopia. He was reunited there with his friend Oliver Tambo. Together they toured northern and western Africa. The growing independence movement then sweeping the continent was a tonic to the struggle-weary South Africans. Everywhere the two men went they recruited young Africans to join in the anti-apartheid struggle.

From Africa, Mandela flew to London to meet with sympathetic leaders of the British Labour and Liberal parties. For the first time in his life, Nelson Mandela came to know what true freedom was. No sharper condemnation of the cruelty of apartheid can be found than this simple, poignant statement: "Wherever I went, I was treated like a human being."

But however high the risk, Mandela couldn't stay away long from his homeland. After visiting

Mandela stands in front of London's Westminster Abbey during a secret trip to England in 1962. His ability to slip in and out of South Africa, despite police efforts to capture him, earned him the nickname the Black Pimpernel.

Algeria, where he took training in guerrilla warfare, and several countries in East Africa, he came home to Johannesburg. He decided that his best strategy was to "hide in plain sight" and moved into a house directly across from the police station.

One day he went to the Rivonia house to see Winnie. She was on her way to their appointment, but a police cordon blocked the road. Desperate to see her husband, she arranged to have an ambulance with a doctor inside drive her through the roadblock. When police stopped the ambulance, they were told the woman inside was in labor. Winnie got through without a problem. It would be the last time she would be alone with her husband for twenty-two years.

Next Mandela met with his old comrade and ANC leader Albert Luthuli, who nine months before had been awarded the Nobel Prize for Peace. Although Luthuli himself would not engage in violence, he had allowed Spear's formation. On his return home from accepting the Nobel Prize in Sweden, Luthuli had been banished to Zululand. He later died there under mysterious circumstances. The official story said he was walking along the tracks of a railroad when he was struck and killed by a train.

On August 5, 1962, a quiet Sunday, Mandela set off from Durban to Johannesburg in a car, disguised again as a chauffeur. His passenger was a white friend, Cecil Williams, a theater director. Near the Howick Falls in Natal, Mandela's car was stopped by three carloads of police. They had been tipped off about the car by an informant, now believed to be a Central Intelligence Agency (CIA) agent from the United States. They were told that "someone special" would be in the car, but they had no idea that the man behind the wheel would be Nelson Mandela himself. After seventeen months of living underground, Nelson Mandela was a free man no longer. The Black Pimpernel had been captured at last.

ACCUSED
NUMBER 1

The South African government had waited a long time to get its hands on the country's "most wanted man," and they didn't intend for him to get out of their grasp again.

When Winnie heard the news of her husband's capture from a friend at the Child Welfare office where she worked, she was devastated. "I knew at that time that this was the end of any kind of family life, as was the case with millions of my people—I was no exception," she later said. "Part of my soul went with him at that time."[1]

Mandela was taken to the old Fort prison in Johannesburg to await trial. He knew he couldn't expect to receive justice from the government, but he saw his trial as an opportunity to bring his message to the world. For his first appearance in the courtroom in Johannesburg he wore a lion skin, the traditional dress of a Thembu chieftain. He raised his fist and cried "Amandla!"—which means "power" in Xhosa. The crowd of supporters went wild. One journalist described the defendant that first day in court as "a quiet avenging giant."[2]

The government was afraid that Mandela's many friends would start riots or even help him escape from jail. They moved the trial from Johannesburg north to Pretoria. They thought Mandela's supporters wouldn't make the trip to Pretoria, but to their frustration, hundreds did.

Mandela handled his own defense, and he did it eloquently. Early on in the trial he questioned the very legal process itself. "Why is it that in this courtroom I face a white magistrate, am confronted by a white prosecutor and escorted into the dock by a white orderly?" he asked. "Can anyone honestly . . . suggest that in this type of atmosphere the scales of justice are evenly balanced?"[3]

There was no evidence linking Mandela to the acts of sabotage still taking place across the country. The government did, however, accuse him of inciting the May 31 strike and then leaving the country without valid documents.

"The government set out . . . not to treat with us, not to heed us, not to talk to us, but rather to present us as wild, dangerous revolutionaries, intent on disorder and riot, incapable of being dealt with in any way save by mustering an overwhelming force against us, and the implementation of every possible forcible means, legal and illegal, to suppress us,"[4] Mandela told the court.

Before the verdict was delivered, the presiding magistrate asked Mandela if he had anything further to say. Mandela answered simply that he was guilty of no crime. Nevertheless, he was found guilty on both counts. Sentencing was set for November 7, 1962.

In his final statement to the court Mandela remained proud, unafraid, and unrepentant:

> *Whatever sentence Your Worship sees fit to impose upon me for the crime for which I have been convicted before this court, may it rest assured that when my sentence has been completed I will still be moved, as men are always moved, by their consciences; I will still be moved by my dislike of the race discrimination against my people when I come out from serving my sentence, to take up again, as best I can, the struggle for the removal of those injustices until they are finally abolished once and for all.*[5]

He was sentenced to five years of hard labor. As Mandela was led from the courtroom, he repeated his cry of "Amandla!"—to which his supporters responded, "Tshotsholoza Mandela," meaning "Struggle on, Mandela." Winnie later reiterated this message to reporters: "Our people suffer inside and out of the jails. But suffering is not enough. We must struggle."[6]

Winnie would now face her own struggle. Soon after, she was issued her first banning order. She couldn't leave Johannesburg without permission, set foot in a school, or attend or address a meeting of more than two people.

Mandela puts on a brave face in this picture taken at the time of his 1962 trial.

As for her husband, he was taken to Pretoria Central Prison, outfitted in baggy prison clothes, and put to work sewing mailbags. But this was only temporary. Such a notorious political prisoner could not be kept for long in the general prison population. He was soon transferred to the maximum security prison on Robben Island, 6 miles (10 kilometers) off Cape Town. Here he was kept in solitary confinement.

In June 1963, after months of pleading with authorities, Winnie was given permission to make the 900-mile (1,450-kilometer) journey from Johannesburg to Cape Town to visit her husband—for thirty minutes. Their visit took place in a shack where they talked to each other in English across a double wire mesh. (The prison authorities wouldn't let them speak in Xhosa, a language the guards couldn't understand.)

Winnie returned home, exhausted and distraught, to find that the police had ransacked her home for the second time. Life for her and her two children would soon become a prison without walls.

Although Mandela was behind bars, the work of the Spear of the Nation continued. By the middle of 1963, some two hundred acts of sabotage were reported, only a portion of them actually committed by the Spear. The saboteurs were growing increasingly desperate. One team stole some dynamite from a road construction camp and then went to the local library to research how to use it!

Walter Sisulu was arrested for his ANC activities and sentenced to six years in prison. More fortunate than Mandela, he was released on bail while appealing his sentence and disappeared underground. But his days of freedom were numbered. On July 11, 1963, the security police moved in on the Spear's farmhouse headquarters in Rivonia, probably on a tip from an informer. They captured Sisulu, who was wearing a thin moustache and dyed hair, along with eight other men. Far worse, the police uncovered a wealth of documents linking the ANC leaders to the sabotage. Joe Slovo, abroad at the time, was the only leader of the saboteurs to escape capture. The Spear of the Nation had been broken.

Mandela was also incriminated and was immediately moved back to the Pretoria prison. Already serving a five-year sentence, he was now about to go on trial with the others on charges of sabotage, high treason, and conspiring to overthrow the government. The ultimate penalty, if convicted, was death.

What came to be called the Rivonia Trial began in earnest in December 1963, at the Palace of Justice in Pretoria. Six blacks, including Mandela and Sisulu, two whites, and one Indian were indicted. Four others who were charged broke out of a Johannesburg police station with the help of a bribed guard. Disguised as priests, they eventually fled to England.

Nelson Mandela cut a less imposing figure in court this time. He had lost a good deal of weight on Robben Island but seemed in good spirits. He drew strength from his friends who now shared the dock with him. When asked how he pleaded, he replied firmly, "The government should be in the dock, not me. I plead not guilty."[7]

As in his previous trial, Mandela saw that there was no way justice would be served. The government used false witnesses against the defendants, tried to tar them with the brush of Communism, and accused them of many acts of sabotage the Spear had no part in. The accused made a pact to use the trial as a public platform to make their ideals and beliefs known not just to South Africa but to the whole world.

As the trial proceeded, Mandela, referred to as "accused no. 1," answered each charge with calm eloquence. To the charge that his training in guerrilla warfare in Algeria and elsewhere was in preparation for a revolution, he replied, "All whites undergo compulsory military training, but no such training was given to Africans. It was . . . essential to build up a nucleus of trained men who would be able to provide the leadership which would be required if guerrilla warfare started."*

Addressing the fears of whites if blacks should be allowed to vote and take over the government, he said, "It is not true that the enfranchisement of all will result in racial domination. Political division based on color is entirely artificial and when it disappears, so will the domination of one color group by another. The ANC has spent half a century fighting against racialism. When it triumphs, it will not change that policy."

Mandela concluded his four hours of testimony with these stirring words:

During my lifetime I have dedicated myself to this struggle of the African people. I have fought against white domination, and I have

---

* All the defendants admitted they were guilty of preparing for a guerrilla war but denied they had taken any decision to start such a war.

fought against black domination. I have cher-
ished the ideal of a democratic and free society
in which all persons live together in harmony
and with equal opportunities. It is an ideal
which I hope to live for and to achieve. But if
needs be it is an ideal for which I am prepared
to die. [8]

Soon after, in an editorial, *The New York Times* referred to the Rivonia defendants as "the George
Washingtons and Ben Franklins of South Africa."
In a resolution carried 106 to 1 (the one nay being
from South Africa), the United Nations called for
the "unconditional release" not only of Mandela
and his cohorts, but of all political prisoners in the
country as well.

On June 11, 1964, the head judge delivered
the court's verdict in a succinct three-minute
speech to a crowd in Pretoria's Church Square: "I
am not convinced that the motives of the accused
were as altruistic as they wish the court to believe.
People who organize a revolution usually take over
the government." [9] All nine defendants but one
were found guilty on all counts.* Sentencing was
set to be pronounced the following day.

Mandela, Sisulu, and the others were prepared for the worst—death. Although the charge
of high treason had been dropped due to a lack of
evidence, the death sentence was still a real possibility.

---

* Lionel Bernstein was acquitted but then promptly rearrested on a charge of
breaking an earlier ban.

While black women paraded outside the Palace of Justice carrying banners reading "NO TEARS: OUR FUTURE IS BRIGHT," the convicted men faced the judge and waited to hear their fate. "I have decided not to impose the supreme penalty," the judge said. "Consistent with my duty that is the only leniency which I can show. The sentence in this case of all the accused will be one of life imprisonment."[10]

The judge's leniency undoubtedly owed as much to world public opinion as any personal compassion. International disapproval of the trial had already led to the start of some sanctions, or economic boycotts, against South Africa. The execution of these men would only further stain the already tarnished reputation of South Africa in the world community.

One English reporter described Winnie this way as she left the courthouse: "She flashed a smile that dazzled. The effect was regal and almost triumphant . . . the crowds of Africans thronging Church Square . . . loved it. They cheered, perhaps the only time black people have ever summoned the courage to cheer in that place."[11]

Mandela was sent back to Robben Island with his six black colleagues. The one white convicted, Dennis Goldberg, was sent to Pretoria Prison. The rules of apartheid applied even to convicted prisoners. Nelson Mandela had faced his last trial. He and the others knew that a life sentence in South Africa held no hope of parole. Barring a miracle, he would live out the rest of his days in prison.

PRISON WALLS

Seals and penguins had once been the sole residents of Robben Island. (The Dutch word *robbe* means "seal" in English.) But since the 1650s, the rocky isle at the mouth of Table Bay had been a prison of one sort or another. At first, the white settlers banished rebellious African chiefs there. Later, it became a leper colony. Still later, it served as a prison for common criminals. Shortly before Mandela's arrival, Robben Island first welcomed a special kind of prisoner—political prisoners guilty of fighting against apartheid.

Nelson Mandela and his seven colleagues faced their grim sentence with the conviction of their beliefs. *They* knew they were not criminals but freedom fighters, opposing an unjust and tyrannical system.

As Winnie Mandela, herself no stranger to prison, has said, "It has become part and parcel of city life for a black to be in and out of jail. No longer is there any stigma attached to it. In fact the opposite applies. A family in which no member has ever been imprisoned is highly suspect—they must surely have come to some arrangement with the police to report others in exchange for immunity!"[1]

On his first stay on Robben Island, Mandela had been alone. Now he would be able to share his hardships with Walter Sisulu and his other ANC comrades. Their bond of friendship and common purpose would sustain and nourish them in the dark days ahead.

Life on Robben Island was an ordeal from their arrival. The men were placed in Ou Tronk, the "old jail," and then moved to a new maximum security section that they helped finish building. A 30-foot (9-meter) wall isolated them from the rest of the prison population. Each of the eighty-eight cells in this section was 7 feet (about 2 meters) square. The furnishings consisted of a mat and two blankets. A forty-watt bulb provided the only illumination. Their diet was made up of porridge, corn, coffee, and a bland soup occasionally enriched by tiny bits of meat or vegetable. The laws of apartheid applied even in this area. Colored and Indian prisoners received a spoonful of sugar with their morning porridge. African prisoners got only half a spoonful of sugar.

One prison tradition allowed prisoners a brief time each Saturday morning to air any grievances. Nelson Mandela, now denied any way to help his cause on the outside, decided to turn his energies to improving life inside the prison. He told prison officials that they should be given useful work to perform, warmer clothes to wear, and better food to eat. He complained that prisoners did not have enough blankets to keep warm on chilly winter nights, or any exercise outside their cramped cells.

Many prisoners believed that his complaints would fall on deaf ears, but after several weeks the men were marched outside into the prison yard and put to work. Their task was to break up large rocks into gravel with hammers. It was a small victory, perhaps, but one that proved Mandela had not lost his ability to persuade and bring about change—even in prison. The only photograph shown publicly of Mandela during his years on Robben Island was taken at this time. It shows him taking a break from crushing stones with Walter Sisulu.

When summer came, the work detail moved outside the prison walls to the lime quarry in the center of the island. Here the men labored daily, digging out limestone, cutting it into slabs, and then loading the slabs onto trucks. In the intense summer heat, the quarry became a hellhole. White lime dust covered the men's bodies, getting into every pore and irritating the eyes. If caught talking, a prisoner would be punished by losing three meals. If caught a second time, he lost six meals.

For Mandela, now in his late forties, the grinding work, combined with poor food and bad living conditions, took a terrible toll. One day he was unable to lift the slabs to the truck and ignored a

Mandela talks with fellow prisoner and ANC colleague Walter Sisulu during a break from crushing stones in the courtyard at Robben Island prison. This is the only photograph of Mandela to be released during the eighteen years he spent on the island.

guard's order to do so. He was accused of being lazy and sent into solitary confinement for six days. His only nourishment was water in which rice had been boiled.

But Mandela would not be broken. Even when his body was weak, his spirit remained strong. When his further complaints went un-answered, he organized the other prisoners in hunger strikes and work slowdowns. These demonstrations won them modest but important rights that improved their lives—hot water for washing, time for recreation both in and out of their cells, a table and bench in each cell, a monthly movie, and probably the most cherished right of all, increased visitations.

From the start, visits were seen as a mixed blessing. The joy of seeing a loved one had to be measured against the humiliating circumstances of the visit itself. On Winnie's first visit after the life sentence, several guards stood watching over each of them as they stared at one another through a tiny, filthy window. Unable to even touch each other, Nelson and Winnie spoke in English through a telephone. Their every word was listened to and recorded. When the thirty-minute visit ended, the warden cried "Time up!" Nelson returned to his cell, and Winnie left for her long journey back to Johannesburg.

Another demand granted the prisoners was the right to study. Mandela started working toward another law degree by correspondence from the University of London. But the only textbooks he was allowed were so out-of-date that he had to abandon his law course and turn to the study of economics.*

When not working or studying, the men found other ways to pass the time. Sisulu played his favorite game—Scrabble. Mandela tended a small garden of vegetables and flowers. Another prisoner cared for pigeons. A fourth collected books.

---

* Getting any kind of reading material in prison was difficult. All newspapers were strictly forbidden. When paper clippings smuggled in by visitors were found in Mandela's cell, he was immediately punished.

In November 1971, Mandela and his fellow inmates were taken off quarry work and assigned to collecting seaweed on the beach to be used for fertilizer. Although the work was still arduous, Mandela was far happier. Now he could breathe the fresh air, feel the sea breeze on his back, and gaze out at the blue ocean. He watched ships pass by and longed to be on one of them, headed for freedom.

In early 1973, Australian journalist David McNicoll was allowed to interview Robben Island's most famous prisoner. Mandela told him, "Things have improved. Diet and clothing are better . . . On this island we abound in hope . . . I know that my cause will triumph."[2]

This interview and others kept Mandela's name and image alive abroad. But in South Africa he was a "non-person." His writings, his picture, and even his name could not be spoken or seen in public. Yet his memory and words would not die. For many blacks, he was now a symbol of the anti-apartheid cause. His very physical absence turned him from an ordinary human being into something of a legend. The government decided to try to pull Mandela down from his pedestal.

In December 1973, Jimmy Kruger, the minister of prisons, came to Robben Island to deliver a message from the government to Mandela and his colleagues. He told them that if they would acknowledge the homeland state of the Transkei, Mandela's birthplace, and agree to live there quietly, they would be pardoned and released. Mandela realized that if he agreed to this, his effectiveness as a leader against apartheid would be over. He would be selling out to the white government and abandoning all his principles. His reply to Kruger was crisp and to the point: "The policy of separate development is wholly unacceptable."[3]

While Mandela was dealing with life in prison, Winnie was facing her own personal ordeal. Before the Rivonia Trial, she had always been surrounded by support—if not from Nelson, then from his colleagues in the ANC. Now, for the first time in her young life, she was entirely alone. She had to face not only the grim fact that she might never have her husband back, but also the reality that everyone—both her enemies and friends—were watching her every move. Would she prove a leader of the anti-apartheid campaign in her own right, or would she show herself to be, as with some other wives of powerful men, simply a "political ornament"?

Gradually, with the help of a liberal Anglican priest, Winnie came to rely on her own strengths as an individual and find her own identity.

Her commitment to her cause would be put to the severest test in the months and years ahead. In 1965, she was placed under a stringent banning order that restricted her to Orlando. She was unable to go to work and lost her job with the Child Welfare Society. With two children to support and no money, Winnie had to find whatever job she could. She worked in a shoe repair shop, a furniture store, and other small businesses. But the police were always at her heels, intimidating her employers until they were forced to fire her. Friends that tried to help were harassed and even put in jail. Her elder daughter, Zeni, was expelled from so many schools that in 1967 Winnie sent her to Swaziland, where she could continue her education without further interruption.

In May 1969, along with twenty-one others, Winnie was arrested for alleged terrorism and placed in solitary confinement in Pretoria Central Prison. The next nine months were an unrelenting nightmare of psychological and physical abuse. But Winnie held fast to her beliefs. When offered her freedom if she would publicly urge those members of the outlawed ANC still at large to surrender, she refused.

In early 1970 she and the other defendants were acquitted but then detained again on similar charges. In September, she was acquitted a second time. A new five-year ban virtually put her under house arrest each evening and on weekends. By the late 1970s, arrest and detainment had become a way of life for Winnie Mandela. She kept a suitcase packed with essentials by the front door so she'd be ready night or day for the "knock on the door."

But Winnie found herself unprepared for the government's next action. In May 1977, she was banished "indefinitely" to the rural town of Brandfort in the Orange Free State. Winnie called the tiny shack in the black ghetto where she was forced to live with daughter Zindzi "a living grave." There was no indoor toilet or running water. She was far from home with no friends to support her. The police continued to harass her. For Winnie Mandela life had reached bottom.

On June 16, 1976, the prisoners on Robben Island were puzzled when the hot water was abruptly shut off during their showers. Mandela sensed this wasn't just another trick on the part of the prison guards, but that something serious had happened outside the prison walls. He was right, although he didn't know it at the time.

In the Johannesburg township of Soweto that day, black students had been demonstrating by the thousands against a new law. The law dictated that Afrikaans would now be the second official language, after English, for teaching in black schools. The students were tired of being told what to do and considered Afrikaans the racist language of their white masters.

During the demonstration in Soweto, a tear-gas grenade was thrown into the growing crowd by a panicky policeman. Another officer fired a single shot. The crowd reacted with fear and then anger. Students threw stones at the police, who then opened fire on them. Two demonstrators lay dead, and a dozen more were wounded.

In the sixteen years since Sharpeville, black African frustration and fear had grown. Now it exploded into fierce hatred. Angry black students built barricades to keep back the advancing police, attacked a government building, murdered two workers inside, and looted and burned. By the next day the death toll had risen into the hundreds, and 139 buildings lay in ashes. One reporter flying overhead in a helicopter said he felt as if he were a "war correspondent flying over a city after a bomb attack." In a speech Prime Minister John Vorster told his Parliament that order would be maintained at all costs.

These tragic events, known as the Soweto uprising, shocked the world. The South African government braced itself for serious economic consequences in world trade. But Nelson Mandela was not pleased. The very thing he had most feared had come to pass. The people, now largely leaderless, had turned to violence to fight violence, without channeling their anger into some constructive path that would ultimately end apartheid.

Yet Mandela would not give in to despair. When his daughter Zeni came to visit him in June 1978 with her husband, the son of the king of Swaziland, and their one-year-old daughter, he was overjoyed. It was his first "contact" visit allowed since he arrived on the island. He held his grandchild—his fifth—in his arms and named her Zaziwe—"hope" in Xhosa.

A month later, Mandela celebrated his sixtieth birthday and his fourteenth year in prison. It was an event noted around the world. Birthday greetings came in bundles to Winnie's humble Brandfort home. Nelson Mandela had not been forgotten. Each day he remained behind prison walls, his reputation was growing stronger and more powerful.

FREE MANDELA!

In September 1978, there was a change of government in South Africa. John Vorster, who had been prime minister for twelve years, stepped down from power when his administration was rocked by a corruption scandal. In the election that followed, Pieter Willem Botha, who had served as minister of defense in the Vorster government, emerged as the new prime minister.

Despite his credentials as a staunch defender of apartheid, Botha had more political savvy than his predecessor. He realized that since the Soweto tragedy, South Africa was becoming more and more of a pariah in the international community. While this was something the old Boers might have relished, the more knowing politicians in the National Party* knew that South Africa could only suffer economically for its policy of separateness.

* The Nationalist Party was renamed the National Party in 1951.

Apartheid was becoming more and more impractical a system, something that Mandela had prophesied more than twenty years earlier. Whatever his intentions, by temperament and background Botha was ill equipped to fulfill the role of reformer.

Meanwhile, more and more attention was being focused on the one man whom many blacks saw as the only hope for South Africa's future. On March 20, 1980, Witwatersrand University, Mandela's old alma mater, launched a "Free Mandela" campaign. Within two months, 58,000 South Africans—both black and white—signed petitions that called for the release not only of Nelson Mandela but of all political prisoners in South Africa. The United States and Europe supported the campaign with enthusiasm.

The timing couldn't have been better. Oliver Tambo, the ANC leader in exile, declared 1980 the "Year of Action" to commemorate the twenty-fifth anniversary of the Freedom Charter. In June, the UN Security Council joined in the growing chorus for Mandela's release in order that "meaningful discussion of the future of the country" could begin.

Back on Robben Island, Mandela's stature continued to grow. In the aftermath of Soweto, a new generation of young black activists joined the island's prison population. To them, Nelson Mandela was an elder statesman in their struggle against apartheid. He was their teacher, their friend, their father. He always had time to talk to any one of them, and more important, he listened to what they had to say.

*The grassroots protest movement to "release Mandela"
gained momentum in the 1980s. This peaceful protest
march, attended by thousands, took place in downtown
Johannesburg in October 1989.*

"Mandela taught me how to survive," recalls Eddie Daniels, a younger prisoner at Robben. "When I was ill, he could have asked anybody else to see to me. He came to me personally."[1]

Mandela, however, certainly had his own share of sorrows. While he was on the island, his mother and his eldest son, Thembi, both died within a year of each other. Winnie applied for permission for him to attend his mother's funeral, but it was denied. He was informed of his son's death in a car crash by the commandant, who called him into his office. Mandela returned to his cell and shared his grief with Walter Sisulu.

Mandela relied heavily on the precious letters from his loved ones to raise him from his depression. In a letter to Winnie dated October 26, 1978, he wrote:

> *I have been fairly successful in putting on a mask behind which I have pined for the family, alone, never rushing for the post when it comes until somebody calls out my name . . . Letters from you and the family are like the arrival of summer rains and spring that liven my life and make it enjoyable. Whenever I write you, I feel that inside physical warmth, that makes me forget all my problems. I become full of love.[2]*

The love Mandela extended to his fellow prisoners did not escape the notice of prison officials. What alarmed them most was the way he unified them intellectually. He encouraged the younger prisoners to continue their education and helped many go back to school. They took the same correspondence courses he himself had started years earlier. He even used funds sent from the outside by friends and supporters to set up an in-prison course of study. The prisoners humorously referred to Robben Island now as "Mandela U." The government decided this free exchange of ideas had to stop. It also felt the growing pressure from around the world to improve conditions for its most famous prisoner.

On the night of April 1, 1982, Mandela, Sisulu, and three of their comrades from Rivonia received orders to pack their few belongings. Under cover of darkness, the men were transported by boat to the mainland. On their arrival in Cape Town, they were herded into a closed army truck and taken, standing, to Pollsmoor Maximum Security Prison in the white suburb of Takia. After eighteen years on the island, Nelson Mandela's imprisonment was about to enter a new phase.

Life at Pollsmoor was both better and worse than on Robben Island. The new prison was far larger and more impersonal than the old cell block. There was no ocean or beach nearby to raise the prisoners' spirits. The high prison wall cut out all signs of nature except for the blue sky overhead.

On the other hand, the quality of life was greatly improved. Rules on reading materials were far more lax. The men could read one English-language newspaper and *Time* magazine regularly and could listen to the radio. Even the food was better. Best of all, prison officials allowed them regular contact visits with family and friends. After twenty-two years of staring at each other through a dirty window, Nelson and Winnie could now kiss and embrace.

Winnie was not Nelson's only visitor. Near the end of 1984, Lord Bethell, a visiting member of the British Parliament, was allowed to visit Mandela in his third-floor dormitory cell. The government's reason for allowing the visit was to let the world see that their most famous prisoner was not being mistreated and was in good health. Mandela was allowed to discuss politics for the first time. He took full advantage of the opportunity. "The armed struggle was forced on us by the government," he insisted to his visitor. "And if they want us now to give it up, the ball is in their court. They must legalize us, treat us like a political party and negotiate with us."[3]

Bethell later compared Mandela with the jailers who surrounded him: "A tall lean figure with silvering hair . . . he . . . seemed like another general in the South African prison service. Indeed his manner was the most self-assured of them all and he stood out as obviously the senior man in the room. He was, however, black."[4]

Mandela proudly showed Bethell his tiny vegetable garden—oil drums in which he raised tomatoes, broccoli, beans, and strawberries. As Bethell left the prison, his gracious host smiled sadly and said, "This is my frontier, this is where I must leave you."[5]

But other visitors were soon to follow. Although Senator Edward Kennedy, a leader of the anti-apartheid campaign in the United States Congress, was denied a visit on a 1985 trip to South Africa, an American lawyer and his wife were allowed to visit and interview Mandela.

The lawyer, Samuel Dash, described Mandela on their meeting this way: "He appeared vigorous and healthy, with a calm, confident manner and dignified bearing that seemed incongruous in our prison surroundings . . . I felt that I was in the presence not of a guerrilla fighter or radical ideologue, but of a head of state."[6]

Publicity like this only enhanced Mandela's image abroad. Far from an embittered victim of injustice, he appeared to be a man filled with passion, confidence, and even good humor. Prison had not broken him; it had only strengthened his resolve and transformed him into a shining hero of almost mythic proportions.

Universities in England and the United States showered him with honorary degrees. Streets and parks in English towns were named after him. Even an atomic particle discovered at Britain's Leeds University was named in his honor.

If South Africa ever needed such a hero, it was now. Violence had become a daily fact of life. Prime Minister Botha's feeble attempts at reform proved disastrous. In 1985 he extended the vote only to coloreds and Indians, enraging the African majority and setting off a new wave of riots and bloodshed. In two years some five thousand people were killed. A state of emergency was declared to contain the violence. Reporters were forbidden to enter troubled areas. Censorship prevented the country and the outside world from knowing what was going on.

Botha's tough stance was not reassuring, however, to many whites, even within his own party. One Johannesburg newspaper claimed, "With the eyes of the world on him, he [Botha] behaved like a hick politician."7

Mandela sent a message to Botha saying he would call a halt to the violence if the government agreed to legalize the ANC again. Botha, ignoring the offer, replied that he would agree to release Mandela if he would publicly renounce violence and agree to settle down and stay put on the Transkei "homeland." It was virtually the same offer made by Vorster six years earlier. Once again, Mandela rejected it flatly. His release would have to be unconditional, he declared.

In an address before the South African House of Assembly, a stung Botha said, "It is . . . not the South African government which now stands in the way of Mr. Mandela's freedom. It is he himself. The choice is his. All that is required of him now is that he should unconditionally reject violence as a political instrument."8

Mandela's response was quick in coming. On February 10, 1985, his daughter Zindzi, now a published poet and a celebrity in her own right, read his statement to a massive crowd in Soweto:

I am surprised at the conditions that the government wants to impose on me. I am not a violent man . . . It was only . . . when all

Zindzi Mandela, Nelson's youngest daughter, is carried on the shoulders of ANC supporters during a demonstration in 1985. Later she read a statement from her imprisoned father rejecting an offer of release from South African president Botha.

other forms of resistance were no longer open to us that we turned to armed struggle. Let Botha show that he is [different from his predecessors]. Let him *renounce violence. Let him say that he will dismantle apartheid . . .*

Only free men can negotiate. Prisoners cannot enter into contracts . . . I cannot and will not give any undertaking at a time when I and you, the people, are not free. Your freedom and mine cannot be separated. I will return.[9]

That promise at times seemed in doubt—not just because of the life sentence, but also because of Mandela's health. Now in his late sixties, he no longer had a robust body. In November 1985, Mandela was operated on for an enlarged prostate. Three years later he nearly died from a bout with tuberculosis.

Botha faced a perplexing dilemma regarding his country's most famous prisoner. If Mandela should die in prison, the people would proclaim him a martyr. If the government released him unconditionally, it would appear to be weak and at his mercy.

Botha chose a third course. He moved Mandela a second time. In December 1988, he was transferred to Victor Verster Prison Farm near the town of Paarl, 40 miles (64 kilometers) from Cape Town. It was a far cry from the stark conditions at Robben Island.

Mandela moved into a three-bedroom farmhouse that overlooked a vineyard. The prison had recreational facilities, including a swimming pool. Mandela had access to a telephone and even a fax machine. Foreign visitors came regularly to pay homage to him. His compound was a nerve center where he received information and stayed in constant communication with his friends and supporters on the outside. Yet all this did not make up for the loss of his companions, who stayed behind in Pollsmoor. Of all the time he spent in prison, this period would prove the loneliest.

Winnie Mandela, on the other hand, had returned to friends and family in Soweto after her long, painful exile in Brandfort. The years of persecution had changed her, however. She was hardened and more militant, in ways that were disturbing. Winnie surrounded herself with bodyguards, young black men who owed their complete allegiance to her and the more radical elements within the ANC. Her behavior earned her the censure of former friends within the organization who had previously held her in the highest respect. Her militant stand would soon have more serious repercussions.

Meanwhile, it was becoming more and more apparent to the people of South Africa and the world that the true prisoner in South Africa was not Nelson Mandela but the white government. It was shackled to its own chains of apartheid, and they were dragging the nation down into economic and social catastrophe.

One clear sign of this was the strengthening of sanctions against South Africa by the United States and numerous other nations. Sanctions are economic boycotts that are imposed by one country on another. By refusing to trade and do business with South Africa, the U.S. government was sending a strong message to the whites in power that apartheid was not to be tolerated and must end. It was hoped that economic hurt would force South Africa to end apartheid, if not on moral grounds, for more practical, selfish reasons.

The other side of this argument was that sanctions would hurt the very people they were set up to help—the black majority. Sanctions would depress the economy and take jobs and necessary

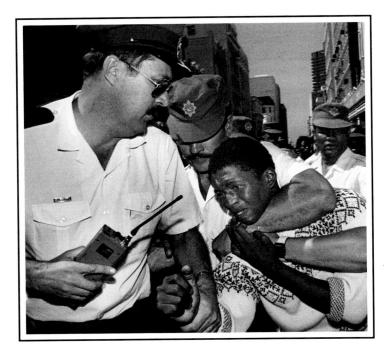

*The white South African government's policy of suppressing
all dissent helped turn world opinion against it. Here a
black youth is arrested by white police following
a meeting to protest increases in bread prices.*

goods away from these already hard-pressed people. This argument was used by both President
Ronald Reagan and British prime minister Marga-
ret Thatcher to justify their stand against sanctions
for South Africa. But the majority of black South
Africans strongly favored sanctions. For them, the
collapse of apartheid was more important than the
temporary suffering sanctions might cause.

Despite Reagan's veto, a Democratic majority
in Congress did make some sanctions law in 1986.
So did Britain's Parliament; other European na-

tions, such as Denmark and Sweden, continued a complete ban on trade with South Africa.

Prime Minister Botha faced other problems at home besides sanctions. He launched a multi-front attack on ANC bases within and without the country, but this only strengthened the organization abroad as more activists fled into exile to other African states.

To stabilize the situation, Botha turned to the one person who could help him, the most influential black in South Africa—Nelson Mandela. Talks commenced between Mandela and a team of high-level government officials to find a common ground for negotiations. After three years, the talks culminated in a forty-five-minute meeting between Mandela and Botha in July 1989. But the results of this meeting were disappointing. Much tea was drunk, but little of value was said. Botha was too close to apartheid and its past to meet Mandela halfway.

Many whites, whatever their political stance, were coming to the grim conclusion that if South Africa was to have a future, it must abandon apartheid and share power with the black majority. The critical question now was how they were going to share power without losing it altogether.

After twelve years in office, Botha had no workable solution to the dilemma. Rumored to be in poor health, he reluctantly stepped down as leader of his party. An election was held in September, the results of which would signal a fresh chapter in the turbulent history of South Africa and the life of Nelson Mandela.

A NEW
BEGINNING

On September 20, 1989, Frederik Willem de Klerk became the new prime minister of South Africa. At first glance, De Klerk hardly seemed promising material for a reformer of his country's apartheid policies.

A fourth-generation Afrikaner, the fifty-three-year-old De Klerk grew up in the conservative white North Transvaal. He had served the National Party for eighteen years as a cabinet member. In all that time he had demonstrated no flair for leadership. Even his older brother Willem, a liberal journalist, admitted he was "always a conformist."[1]

However, like Mikhail Gorbachev, the new leader of the Soviet Union who had come to power a few years earlier, De Klerk was a different breed from the men who preceded him in power. He was only twelve at the time the policy of apartheid was formed in 1948 and had no deep emotional ties to it. Because of this, he could view his country's situation more pragmatically. De Klerk was also more intellectually in touch with the wider world outside South Africa, and what he saw there gave him reason to pause.

Like millions of other white South Africans who had come of age in the 1950s and 1960s, De Klerk saw how apartheid was draining his country—economically, socially, and politically. Apartheid had made South Africa a pariah in the world community, a situation many could see would not change until the system was dismantled. Whatever fears most whites had of domination by the black majority, their fears of economic ruin and a bloody civil war were far greater.

In October 1989, De Klerk began the process of reconciliation with the black community of South Africa and, more specifically, the African National Congress. He signed the release of Walter Sisulu and the other Rivonia prisoners—with one exception. Nelson Mandela remained behind bars.

As the leader of his cause, Mandela's case would be handled more cautiously. Mandela was more than a leader of the armed struggle against apartheid; he was a symbol to millions of people the world over. The prime minister hoped that Mandela would renounce violence before being released.

On December 13, De Klerk met for the first time with Mandela in Cape Town at the presidential residence. This was no trivial tea party, but the first of a series of substantive meetings to negotiate for a new constitution that would replace apartheid with true democracy. The two men seemed to respect each other. Afterward, De Klerk called Mandela "a man of integrity, a man you can trust." Mandela referred to the prime minister as a "man he could do business with."[2]

De Klerk's opening-day speech before Parliament on February 2, 1990, came like a lightning bolt in the dark night of South African history. He announced the legality of the ANC, which had been banned for thirty years, along with sixty other opposition groups. He suspended all executions pending revision of the laws on capital punishment. He pledged to relax the state-of-emergency regulations and to soon release Nelson Mandela from prison unconditionally.

"The season of violence is over," De Klerk announced to the world. "The time for reconstruction and reconciliation has arrived."[3]

While the reforms were joyously welcomed by the black majority, it was the release of Mandela himself that was most eagerly anticipated. Mandela was seen, by both blacks and whites, as the one person who could unite black South Africans, turn them away from violence, and negotiate a meaningful settlement with the government.

However, De Klerk still saw obstacles in the way of Mandela's release. He said he was concerned for Mandela's safety from "the far left and the far right," who saw him as an enemy or an obstacle.

In addition, De Klerk faced opposition from the influential Conservative Party, which had broken away from the more moderate National Party and had won thirty-one percent of the white vote in the last election. The Conservatives wanted apartheid to remain firmly in place and looked on De Klerk as a traitor to his own cause. As for the more moderate majority of white South Africans, De Klerk had to convince them that they could share power with the blacks without losing it entirely. He insisted that white domination would end, but not be exchanged for black domination.

As the warm days of February passed one by one, exhilaration was tempered by second thoughts. Would Mandela actually be released "soon" or would he remain in prison for months, even years? Winnie Mandela herself had her doubts about De Klerk's sincerity.

Then, on February 11, the incredible happened. Nelson Mandela walked out of Victor Verster Prison a free man after twenty-seven years, six months, and seven days of imprisonment. Across the country and the world, the news was greeted with jubilation. In the United States, the Bush administration said it was "very pleased and encouraged" by the news.

Prisoner No. 466/64 suddenly became the most powerful black leader in South Africa. The leadership of the ANC, still in exile in Lusaka, Zambia, quickly elected him their deputy president. Oliver Tambo, ANC president, had suffered a stroke in August 1989 and was still recuperating.

Mandela shakes hands with the man who unconditionally freed him, South Africa President De Klerk. The handshake followed three days of constructive talks between the government and the ANC in May 1990.

After years of dormancy, the ANC was in a state of crisis, and at this critical moment Mandela was seen as the only person who could bring the organization together and deal with the white government.

Just as important, Mandela was to serve as an "ambassador at large," bringing the ANC's message to the world and raising funds to help the struggle against apartheid. Mandela had no illusions. For all his talk and goodwill, De Klerk had done almost nothing yet to end racial discrimination in South Africa. "The pillars of apartheid are still in place," Mandela noted.

On March 2, Mandela began a two-week, four-country tour. He traveled to Zimbabwe, Tanzania, and Ethiopia. His last stop was Sweden, where he met for the first time in twenty-eight years with his old friend Oliver Tambo, who was recovering from his stroke at a Stockholm clinic. It was an emotional reunion.

But the world beyond Africa was clamoring for a look at South Africa's most famous citizen. In March, Mandela visited England and spoke at Wembley Stadium to an enthusiastic audience of 72,000 following a rock concert in his honor. His message was clear—keep your sanctions on South Africa in place. Only by keeping the pressure on will true change come about.

Back home, there were other positive developments. On March 21, the African state of Namibia, formerly South-West Africa, gained independence after seventy-five years of domination by South Africa. Soon after, Joe Slovo, Mandela's old comrade and head of the South Africa Communist Party, returned home. He would be one of the two whites in the ANC's eleven-member delegation to the government talks.

After several delays, the talks finally began on May 2, 1990. Mandela noted the historic nature of the occasion: "This is the first time in seventy-eight years that a truly serious meeting takes place between delegations of the ANC and the succession of white governments that have ruled our country for generations."[4]

Each side had its own agenda to press. The ANC wanted the four-year-long state of emergency lifted, amnesty granted to all political prisoners and exiles, and political trials abolished. The government wanted the ANC to abandon once and for all the guerrilla fighting that had begun under the Spear of the Nation nearly thirty years earlier.

Perhaps as important as the discussions themselves was the human element. After years of enmity, members of the ANC and the government found to their great surprise that their counterparts were, after all, human beings much like themselves. Walter Sisulu found Minister of Law and Order Adriaan Vlok to be a rather pleasant man. Vlok commented to the press that the ANC delegation "were very nice people."

At the end of the three-day session, a joint committee was appointed to hasten the repeal of the state of emergency and the release of political prisoners. For its part, the ANC promised to review its commitment to armed struggle. Both sides, as journalist Christopher Wren perceptively noted in *The New York Times*, had "more to lose now by pulling back than by pressing forward, not least because of ill-wishers on their respective flanks who want to see them stumble."[5]

For De Klerk these ill-wishers included not only the Conservative Party but also a plethora of right-wing extremist groups that declared they would rather fight to the death than lose their privileges to a black majority. On the other hand, Mandela had to contend with the Pan-Africanist Congress. This radical organization was the only one among the previously banned groups that was opposed to negotiating with the government. Its members stuck to their belief that guerrilla warfare was the only cure for apartheid.

But more of a threat to Mandela's leadership than PAC was the Zulu group Inkatha Freedom Party and its leader, Chief Mangosuthu Gatsha Buthelezi. Among black leaders, sixty-one-year-old Buthelezi was the only serious rival for Mandela's mantle of power. A charismatic leader in his own right, Buthelezi had originally been a member of the ANC Youth League but had grown disenchanted with that group's gradual move toward radicalism.

As the spokesperson for 1.7 million Zulus, Buthelezi sought compromise, not confrontation, with white South Africa. Whereas Mandela and the ANC called for nationalization of the country's resources, he spoke out for free enterprise and capitalism. Buthelezi opposed not only the use of violence in the anti-apartheid struggle, but even the use of sanctions to overthrow the government. It was no surprise that Buthelezi was looked upon favorably by many whites as a pleasant alternative to Mandela, and by the ANC as a collaborator who was not to be trusted.

The antagonism between ANC and Inkatha supporters erupted into violence in the mid-1980s and accelerated after the release of Mandela. In-

These Inkatha supporters in the Transvaal defiantly wield traditional Zulu weapons after clashes with ANC supporters. More than five thousand people were killed in the factional fighting between the two groups from 1986 through 1991.

stead of working together, the two groups competed for power. The results led to endless bloodshed across the country, nowhere more intense than in Natal Province. There factional fighting between blacks claimed more than four thousand lives from 1986 to 1990. And within the first four months of 1991, over seven hundred people had been killed in South Africa in the factional fighting. Unable to resolve their differences, Buthelezi and Mandela seemed helpless to stop the killing between their people.

While the two black leaders were keeping their distance, De Klerk was off solidifying his new position within the community of Western nations. In May 1990 he toured nine nations of Western Europe, including Britain, France, and West Germany. Earlier in the year he met with U.S. secretary of state James Baker, a move that drew criticism from Mandela, who claimed Baker's meeting with De Klerk enhanced the prime minister's status for no good reason. Despite the promise of reform, little in South Africa had yet changed, Mandela pointed out. "The reality is that I still have no vote," he said, even though he was free from prison after twenty-seven years.

On June 4, Mandela left South Africa for a six-week tour of a dozen countries, including the United States. The stated purpose of the ambitious trip was to tell the people of the world about the political situation in South Africa. Millions of Americans saw it as a chance to see and hear this world-class hero in the flesh and to celebrate his victory.

Nelson and Winnie arrived at John F. Kennedy Airport in New York on June 20, shortly before noon. Their reception in New York City was an outpouring of love and admiration that city had rarely seen before. Police estimated that at least 750,000 New Yorkers saw Mandela on his first day in the United States.

After a forty-car motorcade through black neighborhoods in Brooklyn and Manhattan, Mandela rode up Broadway in a police flatbed truck topped by a bulletproof glass shelter that was comically dubbed the "Mandelamobile." Many people were concerned about the health of the aging celebrity, who had shown signs of tiring easily long before the tour began. Yet Mandela's spirits rose as he saw the love and respect Americans showered on him and his cause.

"I saw a weary seventy-two-year-old man tired from a very emotional day," said welcoming committee coordinator Roy Wilkins. "But when I was running by that security vehicle, I looked up, and the smile on his face was like a child at Christmas."[6]

The historic day ended at Yankee Stadium, where a crowd of 50,000 Americans watched Mandela don a baseball cap and jacket and joke about being "a Yankee." There were other moments of humor that were unintentional. Listening to fans shout the cry of "Amandla," one police officer turned to his companion and asked, "Who is this Amanda, anyway?"[7]

While the overall impression of Mandela was favorable, there were things he said that disturbed many Americans. On an ABC television special hosted by newsman Ted Koppel, an audience member questioned Mandela's open support of such Third World leaders as the Palestine Liberation Organization's Yasir Arafat, Libyan leader Muammar Qaddafi, and Cuba's Fidel Castro. Mandela refused to disavow his support of these men, seen by many as dictators or terrorists. He insisted that their support of the ANC's struggle

The Mandelas and President and Mrs. Bush enjoy a stroll on the White House lawn during Mandela's first visit to the United States, in June 1990. The triumphant tour began in New York City and ended in Los Angeles.

had earned them his unqualified friendship and said that the United States should not demand that its enemies also become the enemies of his people. Mandela's stance led one white viewer to comment, "Mr. Mandela is to be respected, but he's not God."[8]

More important perhaps than his New York visit was Mandela's stop in Washington, D.C., where he had a three-hour working lunch with President George Bush at the White House. Bush assured Mandela that sanctions would not be lifted until all conditions put forth by the U.S. Congress and the ANC were met. For his part, Mandela told the president that all hostilities would cease once the government accepted the ANC's conditions for negotiations.

The American tour, which ended in a $1 million fund-raising dinner and concert for the ANC in Los Angeles, was a personal triumph for Nelson Mandela. At the United Nations, where Mandela had earlier spoken, Governor Mario Cuomo of New York had called him a symbol of hope for the world.

But that symbol was a flesh-and-blood, white-haired man, and hope was on a collision course with cold reality. As the fanfare surrounding Mandela's release was starting to die down, the bright new beginning for South Africa was looking considerably less bright in the harsh light of day.

After a brief meeting with Britain's prime minister Thatcher, Mandela headed homeward, where new problems and old ones were waiting for him.

AN UNCERTAIN FUTURE

On December 29, 1988, four young black men were kidnapped from a Methodist rectory in Soweto and taken to a private home in another part of the township. The incident might have been just another example of the factional infighting that had been flaring up between different black groups in these desperate years before Nelson Mandela's release. But this case was very different. The men who kidnapped the four were body-guards of Winnie Mandela, and the house they took them to was her home.

The four prisoners were verbally abused and physically beaten by their captors. The victims later claimed that Winnie Mandela herself was present and participated. The youngest, fourteen-year-old James (Stompie) Seipei, was accused of being a spy for the police. The other three were accused of allowing themselves to be sexually abused by the white minister they were staying with. They were told they would be beaten until they confessed to these charges. Sometime during this first day of their captivity, Winnie Mandela left the house to go to a meeting in Brandfort in the Orange Free State, where she had previously lived in exile. She did not return to Soweto until January 31, 1989.

On January 6, Stompie Seipei was found dead in a field with his throat cut. The other three men escaped from the house. In May, Jerry Richardson, Winnie Mandela's head bodyguard, was convicted of Stompie's murder and sentenced to death.

These dark deeds hung over the Mandelas like a storm cloud even as they returned home from their triumphant world tour in July 1990. Two months later, Winnie Mandela was formally charged with kidnapping and assault in the case. Proclaiming her innocence, she and her husband looked forward to her trial as a chance to prove that she had played no role in what happened.

The trial began the following February and lasted fourteen weeks. Nelson Mandela, ever the faithful husband, accompanied Winnie to the Johannesburg courtroom each day but did not stay for the proceedings. After years of her support in his trials, now he would stand by his wife when she needed him. President De Klerk said he admired Mandela for his loyalty and refused to comment further on the trial.

When the verdict was handed down on May 13, Winnie Mandela was found guilty of kidnapping and being an accessory after the fact to assault. She was sentenced to six years in prison. In his statement, the judge declared Mrs. Mandela "to be a calm, composed, deliberate and unblushing liar."

"To imagine that all of this took place without Mrs. Mandela as one of the moving spirits is like trying to imagine 'Hamlet' without the Prince,"[1] he said.

The verdict could not have come at a worse time for Nelson Mandela. Only a few days earlier he and De Klerk had announced that they had made "good progress" on a reconciliation over the thorny problem of "black-on-black" violence in the townships. Mandela had spoken of an "unseen hand," possibly members of government security forces, that had helped to set off the factional fighting and might be assisting the Zulus of the Inkatha Freedom Party.

Winnie's conviction tarnished Mandela's reputation with the white government and hurt him in a different way among some blacks. Young black militants, even within the ANC, were growing more restless and radical. Winnie's more radical stand by the mid-1980s was more appealing to these young people than the less confrontational tactics of her statesmanlike husband. Her conviction was seen as a badge of courage and could only make her more popular among the militants, at her husband's expense.

On the other hand, more moderate blacks distanced themselves from Winnie and her radicalism, even before her conviction. In an election of

Inkatha president Gatsha Buthelezi and Mandela at their first meeting, in January 1991. Their efforts to end factional fighting were unsuccessful.

women representatives within the ANC in early 1991, she failed to garner enough votes for office and lost the support of her longtime friend Albertina Sisulu.

Both Mandela and Buthelezi seemed to be losing their grip over their own followers. They finally met for the first time in years in January 1991 and again in March to settle their differences. But their peace accord seemed to have little effect, and the fighting continued unabated. Only the day before Winnie's conviction, one thousand Zulus had attacked a squatter settlement and killed twenty-seven people with machetes, axes, spears, and guns.

Meanwhile, De Klerk had begun to make good on his promises of reform. On his first trip to the United States, shortly after Mandela's visit, De Klerk received a promise from President Bush. Bush told him that if the South African government did more to meet the conditions set by the U.S. Congress, Bush would support the modification or end of sanctions against South Africa.

In February 1991, De Klerk announced before Parliament that he would soon initiate legislation to repeal the Land Acts, the Group Areas Act, and the Black Communities Act. These laws were among the strongest pillars of apartheid. They reserved most land for whites and restricted blacks to the ghetto-like townships. De Klerk even went so far as to suggest that he might repeal the Population Registration Act of 1950 that divided all South Africans according to race. The speech was enough to send pro-apartheid Conservative Party members storming out of Parliament.

But De Klerk, with continued pressure from the ANC and other groups, was good to his word. In June he repealed the major laws of apartheid, including the Population Registration Act. The following month the ANC held its first national conference since its banning in 1960. To no one's surprise, Nelson Mandela was elected unopposed as president, replacing the ailing Oliver Tambo. More surprising was the election of thirty-eight-year-old Cyril Ramaphosa, a moderate union leader skilled in negotiating, to the office of secretary general. The ANC seemed to be responding to De Klerk's positive reform by steering away from the radicalism of some of its younger members and continuing a course of moderation and constructive compromise.

Just five days after Mandela's election, President Bush lifted U.S. economic sanctions in force against South Africa since 1986. He said that a recent release of political prisoners had completed the five conditions laid down by sanction legislation for its repeal and called apartheid's demise "irreversible."

To accelerate South Africa's return to the international community, on the day before Bush's announcement the International Olympic Committee ended a twenty-one-year ban on South Africa's participation in the Olympics. An integrated team of South African athletes would compete in the 1992 Summer Olympics in Barcelona, Spain.

Today hope is once again on the rise in South Africa, but the bloody factional fighting continues unabated. Reform and violence and hope and despair seem to be running neck and neck, making the future still clouded and uncertain.

So what, exactly, lies ahead for South Africa and Nelson Mandela? Some critics say the dismantling of apartheid in the 1990s is "too little, too late." Years of injustice, hatred, and repression have built up barriers that will be impossible to remove before the very fabric of the society breaks down, they claim. The rise of black-on-black violence may well be the logical extension of a system that categorized people by race and tradition and set them against one another. In this respect, the Inkatha-ANC struggle may be the final bitter fruit of apartheid.

These same critics say Nelson Mandela has outlived his effectiveness as a leader. How can a man, they ask, whose political convictions were formed in the 1940s and who had spent the last twenty-seven years in prison begin to understand the realities of the 1990s? But these people forget that one of Mandela's greatest strengths is his ability to stick to a course of action and see it through, no matter what. And his skillful negotiations with De Klerk have shown him to be both an idealist and a pragmatic politician who can get things done.

If Mandela has been brought down from his pedestal, it should be remembered that he never asked to be put up on one. He remains a man of great dignity, but also great modesty. In all the years he has labored for his people's liberation—at great personal sacrifice—he has gained no material rewards. Whereas another man might have come out of prison embittered and hateful, Mandela remains full of love and hope, for enemy and friend alike.

It remains to be seen whether Mandela can adapt to the treacherously shifting political scene and regain some of the influence he has lost since his release from prison. One thing, however, is clear. Without his leadership in the ANC, the mass protests, the rallies, and even the violence that put him behind bars in the early 1960s, the changes in South Africa today would not be taking place. Like a constant drip of water on a rock, Mandela and the ANC have gradually worn down the apartheid system. Their persistence and courage have paved the way for a moderate like De Klerk to emerge and have the power base to change the system. Without Nelson Mandela, civil war and anarchy might have overtaken South Africa years ago. If the possibility of such a threat still lies ahead, there is also the very real hope that it can be averted.

Whatever happens, Nelson Mandela has already earned himself a special place in the history of his country. Thanks to him, change in South Africa, like the changes that have taken place in Eastern Europe, will surely be irreversible. There can be no going back to the repression of the past. The future will bring new and different challenges, some of them just as perplexing.

The majority of South Africans today, both white and black, want a future in which they can live together in peace and prosperity. They have no better role model to achieve these goals than Nelson Mandela. Despite his age, he may still become the first black president of a free and democratic South Africa, or he may prove to be another Moses who sees the Promised Land but does not himself live to enter it. Whatever fate has in store for him, he will not be forgotten, as long as people fight injustice and dream of a better life. Nelson Mandela's walk to freedom has become an irreversible march in which a nation goes forth to meet its destiny.

CHRONOLOGY

1918	Nelson Mandela is born in Qunu, village in the Transkei territory, South Africa (July 18)
1940	Expelled from the University College at Fort Hare for political activities
1941	Arrives in Johannesburg, works at a variety of jobs, meets Walter Sisulu
1944	Joins the African National Congress (ANC), marries Evelyn Ntoko Mase, a nurse
1948	Afrikaner Nationalist Party comes to power, begins apartheid policies in South Africa
1950	Mandela elected national president of the ANC's Youth League
1952	Arrested for breaking curfew and spends first night in jail (June 26)
1953	Banned for first time for six months
1955	ANC and Congress Alliance issue the Freedom Charter (June 25)
1956	Mandela arrested with 155 others on grounds of "high treason" (Dec. 5)

1957	Divorces first wife
1958	Marries Winnie Nomzamo Madikizela, a social worker
1960	Sixty-nine blacks are killed by police in the Sharpeville massacre (Mar. 21) ANC and other anti-apartheid groups are declared unlawful (Apr. 8)
1961	Mandela and remaining defendants in the Treason Trial are acquitted and freed (Mar. 29) Spear of the Nation, sabotage group within ANC, strikes for first time (Dec. 16)
1962	Mandela captured after many months living underground and charged with inciting a strike and other crimes (Aug. 5) Sentenced to five years of hard labor (Nov. 7)
1963	Rivonia headquarters of ANC raided; Sisulu and eight others arrested (July 11) Rivonia Trial begins (Dec.)
1964	Mandela and co-defendants sentenced to life in prison on Robben Island (June 11)
1976	Killing of black demonstrators results in the Soweto uprising (June 16)
1977	After years of persecution and police harassment, Winnie Mandela is banished "indefinitely" to Brandfort in the Orange Free State (May)
1978	Pieter Willem Botha becomes prime minister of South Africa
1980	"Free Mandela" campaign begins at Mandela's alma mater, Witwatersrand University
1982	Mandela, Sisulu, and three other prisoners are transferred from Robben Island to Pollsmoor Prison on the mainland (Apr. 1)

1985	Mandela refuses offer of freedom from Botha with conditions he will "unconditionally reject violence as a political institution" and move to homeland
1988	Transferred to Victor Verster Prison Farm near Cape Town (Dec.)
1989	Frederik Willem de Klerk becomes prime minister and quickly begins reform measures (Sept.)
1990	De Klerk ends thirty-year ban on ANC and other anti-apartheid groups (Feb. 2)
	Mandela freed after twenty-seven years, six months, and seven days of prison (Feb. 11)
	ANC and government representatives meet to negotiate for plans for a new constitution (May 2)
	Mandelas visit the United States and receive an extraordinary welcome (June)
1991	Winnie found guilty of kidnapping and accessory after fact in assault of a young black killed by one of her bodyguards (May 13)
	De Klerk calls for repeal of the Population Registration Act, one of pillars of apartheid system (June)
	Mandela elected president of ANC (July 5)
	President George Bush announces end of most U.S. sanctions against South Africa (July 10)

NOTES

Chapter One

1. Videotape, *Mandela: Free at Last*.
2. Ibid.

Chapter Two

1. Mary Benson, *Nelson Mandela: The Man and the Movement*, p. 21.

Chapter Three

1. Benson, p. 28.
2. Heidi Holland, *The Struggle: A History of the African National Congress*, p. 67.

Chapter Four

1. Holland, p. 69.
2. Benson, p. 39.
3. Ibid. p. 50.
4. *Current Biography Yearbook 1984*, p. 252.
5. Benson, p. 46.
6. *Current Biography Yearbook 1984*, p. 255.
7. Holland, pp. 85–86.
8. Benson, p. 56.
9. Ibid. p. 63.

Chapter Five

1. Benson, p. 66.
2. J.D. Omer-Cooper, *History of Southern Africa*, p. 213.
3. Ibid. p. 75.
4. Holland, p. 114.

Chapter Six

1. Nancy Harrison, *Winnie Mandela*, p. 69.
2. Benson, p. 88.
3. Ibid. p. 104.
4. Ibid. pp. 97–98.
5. Ibid. p. 110.
6. *Newsweek*, Feb. 19, 1990.
7. Holland, p. 132.

Chapter Seven

1. Winnie Mandela, *Part of My Soul Went with Him*, p. 76.
2. Benson, p. 118.
3. Ibid. pp. 120–21.
4. Ibid. p. 127.
5. Ibid. pp. 130–31.
6. Ibid. p. 132.
7. Ibid. p. 138.
8. Ibid. pp. 150–59.
9. Ibid. p. 161.
10. Ibid. p. 163.
11. Allister Sparks, London *Observer*, Mar. 20, 1983.

Chapter Eight

1. Harrison, p. 64.
2. *Current Biography Yearbook 1984*, p. 254.
3. Benson, p. 183.

Chapter Nine

1. Benson, p. 173.
2. Fatima Meer, *Higher than Hope: The Authorized Biography of Nelson Mandela*, p. 334.
3. Benson, p. 229.
4. Ibid. p. 228.
5. Ibid. p. 230.

6. *The New York Times*, July 7, 1985.
7. Benson, p. 243.
8. Ibid. p. 234.
9. Ibid. pp. 236–37.

Chapter Ten

1. *Time*, Feb. 5, 1990.
2. Ibid.
3. *Newsweek*, Feb. 12, 1990.
4. *The New York Times*, May 3, 1990.
5. Ibid. May 6, 1990.
6. Ibid. June 21, 1990.
7. Ibid.
8. Ibid. June 23, 1990.

Chapter Eleven

1. *The New York Times*, May 13, 1991.

BIBLIOGRAPHY

Benson, Mary. *Nelson Mandela: The Man and the Movement*. New York: Norton, 1986.

Harrison, Nancy. *Winnie Mandela*. New York: George Braziller, 1985.

Haskins, Jim. *Winnie Mandela: Life of Struggle*. New York: Putnam, 1988.

Holland, Heidi. *The Struggle: A History of the African National Congress*. New York: George Braziller, 1989.

Hoobler, Dorothy and Thomas. *Nelson and Winnie Mandela*. New York: Franklin Watts, 1987.

Mandela, Nelson. *No Easy Walk to Freedom*. London: Heinemann, 1965.

Mandela, Winnie. *Part of My Soul Went with Him*. New York: Norton, 1984.

Meer, Fatima. *Higher than Hope: The Authorized Biography of Nelson Mandela*. New York: Harper and Row, 1988.

Omer-Cooper, J.D. *History of Southern Africa*. London: James Currey Ltd., 1987.

INDEX

Page numbers in *italics* refer to illustrations.

(127)

Important Event